NEW POETRIES VII

LUKE ALLAN

ZOHAR ATKINS

ROWLAND BAGNALL

SUMITA CHAKRABORTY

MARY JEAN CHAN

HELEN CHARMAN

REBECCA CULLEN

NED DENNY

NEIL FLEMING

ISABEL GALLEYMORE

KATHERINE HORREX

LISA KELLY

THEOPHILUS KWEK

ANDREW LATIMER

TOBY LITT

RACHEL MANN

JAMES LEO McASKILL

JAMIE OSBORN

ANDREW WYNN OWEN

PHOEBE POWER

LAURA SCOTT

VALA THORODDS

NEW POETRIES
7

AN ANTHOLOGY

edited by

MICHAEL SCHMIDT

CARCANET

First published in Great Britain in 2018
by
Carcanet Press Limited
Alliance House, 30 Cross Street
Manchester M2 7AQ

A CIP catalogue record for this book is available from
the British Library, ISBN 9781784105587.

The publisher acknowledges financial assistance
from Arts Council England.

Printed and bound by SRP Ltd.

CONTENTS

Preface

EDITING THE *New Poetries* anthologies is the most pleasurable and testing of my editorial tasks. No fixed schedule governs their appearance. I know a new anthology is taking shape when a particular poem announces, *it's that time again.* The process begins, usually because I have been enjoying some of the new poets in PN *Review* and a quick census tells me there is a chine, a prickle, a surfeit, a blessing – a group – of new poets waiting. Many of Carcanet's first collections take shape in PN *Review* and *New Poetries.*

The poem that set me on the road to *New Poetries V* was 'This is Yarrow' by Tara Bergin; to *New Poetries VI* was 'Slaughterer' by Vahni Capildeo. Laura Scott's 'and Pierre?' was the catalyst for this book.

> With his ripe face like one of those pale freckled pears
> you hold in your hand and his mind shuddering across it
>
> like a bruise – he's legible to all the world. With his great legs,
> broad and strong as the trees, he walks in and out of chapters
>
> smelling of eau de cologne, or an animal that sleeps in a barn.
> With his long fingers running across the stubble on his jaw,
>
> he listens to the black Russian rain before he picks up his pen.
> With his eyes so blue you'd think he'd drunk the sky down
>
> with all that champagne, he watches the soldiers (red epaulettes
> and high boots) drag that boy to the place where they shoot him.
>
> He watches the boy pull his loose coat tight before he sags and slides
> down the post. And when it's all over, he watches them roll him
>
> gently into the hole with the others and before he can look away,
> he sees, there in the earth, the boy's shoulder still moving.

This is not the only Tolstoyan moment in Laura Scott's poems, but it is the most affecting. It also happens to be a sort of couplet sonnet, and readers familiar with earlier *New Poetries* know how partial they are to the sonnet, a recurrent, even a pervasive form in these volumes.

Its mastery of the poet, the poet's mastery of it, the reciprocities of the form, are a kind of editorial proof. Can one be original in it? What can it do that it hasn't done a hundred times before? Can the sonnet genuinely accommodate narrative? Does it (does any lyric) in the post-Culler age dare to risk the preterite? The future tense? Andrew Latimer describes his work in this anthology as starting from a 'sonnetish poem, with its volta acting as dynamo – propelling and organising', which 'makes its material memorable just long enough until it can eventually be scribbled down – during a lunch break, stolen toilet stop'. Several actual and seeming sonnets have found lodging in *New Poetries VII*. James Leo McAskill, a committed sonneteer, says of his poems, 'they are as different as they are similar, and are meant to be read as such'.

Laura Scott's note on her poems speaks for her creative and, by extension, for my editorial stance: 'So the act of making these poems is also an act of submission. To put it schematically: the image has authority, and the writing must defer to it. The poem has to shed some of its busy self-importance, to lose some of its intention, to go quiet. All the poems do, all they can do, is circle the image, go around the outside of it so that it can occupy the space in the middle.' As anthologist I declare, 'the achieved poem has authority, and editing must defer to it.'

Deferring as editor begins when a poem earns its place. I open submission envelopes, glance at covering letters, look over the first poem. In the case of 'and Pierre?' I was compelled to read aloud. The poem insisted not on the poet's but on a reader's voice ('legible to all the world'). Once I began to say it, the poem's prosody, syntax and lineation created anticipation, started generating the variations and surprises that become its drama and its residual magic. Not only the reader experiences this enchantment: the poet too must feel it, standing outside the thing of words she has made. As she re-reads and revises I can imagine her asking, bemused, how language has delivered just *this* poem. The news that stays news, as Pound called poetry, is that recurring sense of surprise. The poem can be read, can read you, a dozen times and provide incremental pleasures. Feeling produced by language, rather than feeling producing language. Some readers set out to memorise poetry. I prefer to learn by heart.

Different as the poems included in this anthology are – from concrete poems to extended philosophical meditations – they share concerns with form and language, issues they resolve differently. Yet there is coherence in this book as in its predecessors, a sense of continuity with the past and the future of the art. Ned Denny talks of the synthesis in his poems and translations, 'the apparent paradox of something both highly ordered and numinous, condensed yet expansive, Apollo and Dionysus in one'. Andrew Wynn Owen writes of 'the mind's capacity, sometimes, for active self-redirection'. Zohar Atkins feels on firmer ground, declaring, 'For me, poetry is the discipline of subverting discipline; it is theory in reverse.' His themes and language are rooted in scripture. So too are Rachel Mann's (she is a member of the Anglican clergy): 'The genesis of my poems in this selection lies, in large measure, in acknowledgement of the ever-failing grip the Word has on a culture once saturated by it.' For Vala Thorrods, 'The spirit dwells in us like a curse or a spell, and these poems try to embody that haunted feeling.'

The poets express the contrariety of art, the bringing into balance that entails different degrees of self-effacement in the making of the thing that is a poem, which exists in its 'fundamental "otherness"' (Jamie Osborne). It is the poems' integrity that makes it possible for them to engage with some of the political realities of our time, as with less time-bound experiences. Sumita Chakraborty's single poem in this book may be 'an elegy of a kind', but 'it was my hope to write the mood of elegy rather than an elegy proper, or to write a way of inhabiting grief rather than exactly writing about grief'. And the poem thus becomes habitable by the reader, an experience rather than a report on experience.

For some of the poets the choice of English is a challenge, to themselves and to the reader; and the choice is never quite complete. Mary Jean Chan, whose poems are political at every level, says, 'I have chosen to write in English, yet Chinese is always there in my work as its foil or fraternal twin, largely owing to the fact that I only speak in Cantonese or Mandarin Chinese with my parents, and my mother does not speak English.' She adds, 'I have experienced how an attentiveness to form – be it a sonnet or pantoum, or simply a tercet or couplet – offers a powerful means to negotiate complex emotions that arise from our lived experiences as social, political and historical beings.'

Rebecca Cullen looks in a different direction, drawing into her poems tones and voices from worlds not immediately her own, as in 'Majid Sits in a Tree and Sings':

> This morning, I wake with a bird in my heart.
> My mother smiles only for me. I bash my car into the wall.
> Sometimes she tells me to be quiet. Today, she laughs.
>
> The men came in the hottest part of the day.
> A walk, my love, a small walk, she says.
> In the stairwell, the mothers hold their children.
>
> The guns shine in the sun. I am a man,
> this is no time for play, I do not hide.
> We shuffle in, look for a seat in the stands.
>
> A big black bird comes down from the sky.
> The grown-ups hold their breath. They are blinking a lot.
> The bird likes the meat hanging on the goalposts.
>
> Tonight, my mother says I can sleep in her bed.
> I make my back into a curved shell against her legs.
> She strokes her palm across my forehead.
>
> In the middle of the night, I watch her on her knees.
> She tips her head backwards. I see all of her neck.

A sonnet could not quite have contained the narrative, though there is a kind of sonnet movement up through the fourteenth line, then the I's perspective changes to register the vulnerability of the 'she' and hence of him (and her) self.

Helen Charman too accepts her vocation as at once poetic and political. 'I think the ongoing work of reconsidering the historical "canon" can help to clarify the challenges of the present.' The re-tuning of the canon, and the loosening of bonds with it, have been at the centre of Theophilus Kwek's adjustment to the contemporary British 'voice', a term to whose treachery he is alert. 'Having grown up with the even cadences of the King James Bible and Shakespeare's plays, I arrived here in 2013 to find a rhythm – of speaking and living – that was more troubling and yet more alive: an urgent, all-embracing pulse that gently remade all my expectations in favour of a younger, more diverse Britain. I quickly found community among those with different accents and persuasions, and lost an initial shyness over my Singaporean voice.'

The surprises that recommend a poem to an editor and then to a reader, and are often its occasion, are identified by Rowland Bagnall. He's 'interested in glitches, particularly when language, sense, and memory go wrong, and in the different ways of using/abusing these malfunctions', and in his anarchic but curiously ordered studio he declares, 'It's possible that my writing has something in common with collage's particular species of vandalism.' He adds, with a touch of rueful realism, 'I like to think of these poems as having nothing to do with me personally, but get the feeling this is not the case.'

What the poets tell us about the occasions for their poems illuminates not only their work but the art more generally, even (or especially) when the information is most particular. Lisa Kelly describes herself as half-Danish and half-deaf. The consequences of the latter are not quite what we might expect:

> I have to work hard to listen and this requires me to place you to my right side, to watch your lips, to watch your hands, to watch your gestures. How can form not matter? To understand what you say, I must attempt to control our interrelated physical space. Of course, I often fail and confusion, mis-interpretation, annoyance, as well as humour are by-products. My poems reflect my obsession with form and the physical space that words occupy on the page.

Isabel Galleymore works in what may seem an unusual way. '[M]uch of my writing starts with research. "Kind" [p. 308], for example, emerged from a day spent at an owl sanctuary where many owls have become "imprinted": a term used, in this case, for animals who become so familiar with humans that they begin to take on certain human behaviours.' Katherine Horrex is similarly particular, and then earns the right to generalise: 'I wanted to acknowledge a set of grim, but interesting environmental truths. Microclimates. Unhelpful forms of education.'

More up-beat, with a strong narrative instinct, is Neil Fleming: 'Also there are stories. Some with pirates in.' Stories are his *metiér*. His 'Clock with Brass Winding Key' (p. 289) concludes,

> But really it's about explaining what happened once,
> And about what will happen later on, long beyond
> Anything we might guess now. About the hours till it's day.

NEW POETRIES VII

LAURA SCOTT

Sometimes images get stuck in my head. They lie across my mind for days, sometimes for weeks and months. And when I try and brush them away they just stay there, like threads of cobweb you can't quite reach that hang from high ceilings. They won't drop into that place of knowledge and recognition where they can be slotted in and understood. They don't want to go there. Instead they stick stubbornly to their own luminous strangeness, refusing to mean. All I can do with them is put them into poems because they will go there. So that's what these poems are – images that got stuck. And sliding them across involves accepting that they will behave in pretty much the same way inside the poem – they won't suddenly sit up and start to mean. They'll just lie there.

So the act of making these poems is also an act of submission. To put it schematically: the image has authority, and the writing must defer to it. The poem has to shed some of its busy self-importance, to lose some of its intention, to go quiet. All the poems do, all they can do, is circle the image, go around the outside of it so that it can occupy the space in the middle.

And once I'd realised that, the actual writing – about a fence, or a man dying in a field, or the sound of a song – was easier than I'd imagined. I'm not saying that writing these poems was easy, but that it was important not to try too hard. Ease is an essential part of it. If the image is there, at the centre of things, then after that it is just a question of detail, of registering it as minutely as I can, bit by bit, so that it can be seen by somebody else. What these poems are, I hope, is a trace of that ease, because without ease there wouldn't be a poem.

If I could write like Tolstoy

                                       you'd see a man
dying in a field with a flagstaff still in his hands.

I'd take you close until you saw the grass
blowing around his head, and his eyes

looking up at the white sky. I'd show you
a pale-faced Tsar on a horse under a tree,

breath from its nostrils, creases in gloved fingers
pulling at the reins, perhaps hoof marks in the mud

as he jumps the ditch at the end of the field.
I'd show you men walking down a road,

one of them shouting to the others to get off it.
You'd hear the ice crack as they slipped down the bank

to join him, bringing their horses with them. You'd feel
the blood coming out of the back of someone's head,

warm for a moment, before it touched the snow.
I'd show you a dead man come back to life.

Then I'd make you wait – for pages and pages –
before you saw him, go to his window

and look at how the moon turns half a row
of trees silver, leaves the other half black.

Tolstoy's Dog

What is it about the lavender-grey dog
   hanging around the men
playing with a piece of straw
   as if it were a stick
while Moscow burns behind them?
   What is it that makes her lie
across my mind as if she might be
   what all those words were about?

and Pierre?

With his ripe face like one of those pale freckled pears
you hold in your hand and his mind shuddering across it

like a bruise – he's legible to all the world. With his great legs,
broad and strong as the trees, he walks in and out of chapters

smelling of eau de cologne, or an animal that sleeps in a barn.
With his long fingers running across the stubble on his jaw,

he listens to the black Russian rain before he picks up his pen.
With his eyes so blue you'd think he'd drunk the sky down

with all that champagne, he watches the soldiers (red epaulettes
and high boots) drag that boy to the place where they shoot him.

He watches the boy pull his loose coat tight before he sags and slides
down the post. And when it's all over, he watches them roll him

gently into the hole with the others and before he can look away
he sees, there in the earth, the boy's shoulder still moving.

Fragment

How can I forget the feel of her ribs
under my fingertips,

the thump of her slow heart
into my hand? I will be the frost

running silver threads through brown leaves under her feet –

The Singing

I heard it in that weirdly wintery room where the velvet curtains
fell in liver-coloured scrolls and crept out from the walls
when they found the floor and the dark wood cabinet waited
in the corner. That was where they sang for us, or for each other,

or for Greece. I'm not sure who – all I know is the sound of it,
its swell and its swoon, the swerve of it as it left their fingers
and throats and pulled the air into new shapes around us.
And if I circle it, slowly, with these lines, go round the outside of it,

some of that sound might slide into your ears. If I told you
what they looked like, the three musicians, the fat one
in the middle with his bald head and his great belly
arranged over his thighs, more like a butcher than a musician,

and the other two sitting impassively on either side, as if they were bored
– then maybe you'd see them sitting there, with the windows
and the velvet curtains behind them. You'd see me in the front row,
shifting in my seat, wondering when they were going to start.

And then you'd watch the bald one thread his hand under the neck
of his guitar and lay the other over its body and start to play
and the sounds of those notes, higher and faster than you'd expect
would fall into the room like leaves as he moves his fingers

quickly over the fret board. And that would be enough, easily enough,
you could sit and listen to the sharp sounds of the strings
climbing the air forever, but then he'd give you his voice as well
and you won't be able to believe that such a voice could come

from such a source. And some bit of you would back away like a horse
rearing up on its hind legs, troubled by something its rider can't see
because you won't know where to put the sound, what to do with it.
And you'll wonder why the other two are there, they're not doing
     anything,

just looking at the floor but they don't look bored anymore. But then
the old one with the slicked-back hair will start to hum, and the sound
will be as deep and dark as the lines on his face. And when the song starts
its ascent, the other man will come in and the three voices will plait

themselves together until the tune is so strong you could climb up it.
And the air will be so taut, you'll hear the breath caught
in the back of your own throat. And then the song will swerve downwards
in its layered refrain and the audience around and behind you

add their voices to the musicians' and all the voices will go down together
as if the song had stairs and they were made of stone
and the voices were like the soles of thousands of shoes lapping away
at the stone year after year until there is a dent in the middle of the step.

And you'll follow them, wishing you knew the words, willing the song
to go on pouring itself into the room. And that layer that locks you
into yourself will fall away and you'll remember Caliban, crying out
when he wakes from his dream and longs to hear that song again.

a different tune

oh my heavy heart how can I
make you light again so I don't have to

lug you through the years and rooms?
Shall I make a sling for you of silk and fingers

in a blue that brings out your bruised red?
I could hang it from the bony strut

of my collarbones to hammock your sad weight.
Would you soften your walls and open

your dark chambers if I did? I'm the one –
the only one – who really loves you

so be light for me, light like the bird
perching on the rose stem, its pronged feet

threaded through the black thorns –
so light the stem barely moves.

What I know

is this   this
              is what I *really* know, this is what tocks
and ticks inside me, this is what seeps out –
              my signature scent, the one that catches
in the fine hairs of your nostrils so you can sniff me out in a room
    full of people.

This is what paper-cuts my throat and clouds the trees
         that grow in the soft bed of my lungs.
This is what I know and what I know is this –
              you've watched me and clocked me and found me
wanting.   That's where I am
         caught here in this smear with you
running your cold carp eyes over my words and recognising their lack,
my lack, my heaving lack, the one I carry on my back –
              that's what I know   that's what I write
while others tweet and fleet in a silver shoal up to the light.

Lines on a broken statue of Iris

What are you
                   a goddess or a servant forever
tied to their purpose?
Iris of my eye   you must be more than that.
              I only saw a fragment of you
         caught   mid-leap in the stone's soft lip
                   the ripples in your robe
blown against your thighs,
                   your wide stride
spanning
         all possible worlds.

Did they make you to embody
their thoughts, to carry their desire
                through air and water, to fall like a stone
down a well to the unseen face waiting in the dark
                        to sound out their message?
Or do you sometimes
                slip your reins
        and turn your body away
                        from their intention?

What the trees do

They play with us
they want to be us
they once were us

a long time ago
one of them
caught the heel of a girl

in the crook of its branch,
snagged it like a bird
caught in a bush

flicked her
up into its leaves.
She cried and the birds

scattered so no-one heard
and the tree pushed her
higher and higher

up to where its branches
scratched the sky
and the wind blew her

hair into the leaves,
up to where the tree
thrummed under her

and the birds' throats
quivered next to her and her ribs
opened and softened

and their tips pushed
through her skin into the bark
and the tree grew around her.

And sometimes you hear her
tapping her fingers
against your window.

They play with us
they want to be us
they once were us.

Turner

His father saw it before anyone else,
the boy could paint light, could take the sky
into the bristles of his brush and lay it flat
like ribbon around a haberdasher's card.

He could take the curl of cloud, the line
of sea, and drop them on to canvas
pinned and waiting for him like a spider's
web on a window pane. He could make

colours his father had never seen appear
in white china bowls, grinding red lead
and smalt, madder and green slate
while his father washed bundles of hair

ready for the next day, rolling them
between finger and thumb, smoothing
the shafts flat as fish scales. In the morning,
when the light was at its sharpest, Joseph lit

the colour with water and gum, stirring in
honey so the Prussian blues and milky greens,
the scarlets and viridians, could breathe across
the hatched threads of the canvas. And while

his father knotted and threaded the hair
into silken caps, weaving it into clusters
of curls, the boy split shafts of light
until they shimmered on the tip of his brush.

And for a moment, the father looked up
from his work and was scared by the boy
who could paint God's light across the water,
the air's joy at being empty handed.

The Dogs in Greece are different

Rumours buzz around them like flies. Some say
they've taken over the old airport in Athens,
roaming its runways, loping around
the abandoned planes, cocking their legs on the clumps
of grass growing through the cracks in the tarmac.
Somebody has actually seen them, sleeping
on the unmoving baggage carousels and chewing
the dead cables, howling under the announcement boards
proclaiming flight details of planes long gone.
There are stories of them guarding the Acropolis at night
in return for scraps of food, of thousands of them
being rounded up and driven away in lorries
before the Olympics, and poisoned or released into the hills,
depending on who you're talking to. They say the ones
in the towns are fine, they spend their days lying in the shade
and their nights strolling around the bars and restaurants.
But the ones at the edges where the roads turn into motorways
and the grass grows tall and thick, they're the ones you have to watch.
They have started to pack and someone has drawn black lines
around their pale lemon eyes. The bitches are always on heat
and the litters are getting bigger. The pups with the soft pink
paw pads are the first to go and soon their own mothers
will be breaking their necks before they've opened their eyes.
And one day a man will come home, dressed as a beggar,
a man who has been travelling for years and years but this time
there will be no dog flattening its ears and thumping its tail
at the sight of him, this time there'll be wolves
circling the scrubland where he swears his house used to be.

To the Trees

quick and slick
     and full of you,
the you I don't want,
       the you that brims over, brims under my lines, the you
                        I can't
remake, reshape,
     the you I –
   just leave it, drop it, walk away. There's nothing to see here.

Go to the trees,
     I always go to the trees, but let's go
to the tree outside my window,
     the one standing on its own, away from all the others,
the one with the great arms stretching up

the one with too many fingers spreading themselves
     into shapes so the fierce birds might come to them. Too many
                    for what?

To be just pointing at the sky,
     to be just making shapes for the birds?

They must be a trace of something,
     of some hand, some principle urging them on –

maybe Maths or God
     and God knows we don't want to go down that road
        do we?

     Just look at the trees.

I wish I didn't know any rules, any at all, and then my poems,
      or this poem at least,
would move, would soar, would hover and break
      into thousands and thousands
           of pieces of white material.

The Thorn and the Grass

That day I ran my fingers over my son's knee
and they slowed as if puzzled by a sudden patch
of hardness where the skin thickened and pulled
me back to trace the contour lines around it. And there
in the middle of his soft flesh that black pin prick
puncturing his creamy skin and my fingers pressing
down on the ridge around it and us watching as a tip slowly
emerged, pushing its nose up into the air. So I pressed
a little harder and this great thorn slid out of his knee,
the unmistakable curve of a rose thorn freed from his flesh.
But then what about the grass, shall I make her the grass
that grows in the cold sand high above the beach,
blown sad and sharp by the wind, swishing her blades
from side to side, waiting for him to run through her?

So Many Houses

When the grown-ups came we scattered like dust
into the skirting boards – and watched
as they swirled and whirled and married the wrong people.

So many rooms and so many houses
they had to spread the paintings
thinly over the walls. We jumped on the beds

and ran in the gardens, climbed all those stairs
curled our fingers around all those banisters
but we stood still on the landings and felt

the floorboards warp under our feet.
All those houses but only one pattern
and they made it again and again as if it were a song

they loved and they had to play again and again,
a song about a girl with skin as white as alabaster
who danced with a man with hair as black as night,

a song about the child he gave her before he left her
to find another who would give her two more
and as we listened to the song coming through the floorboards

it settled into us and we saw ourselves
spread out in a deck of cards across the table,
a fan of children with different coloured hair.

Fence

What is it about the fence that scares me? you know the one
I mean, the one with gaps between its narrow wooden slats
and a length of wire running across its back. Is it the way
it leans and sags into the grass that grows on the dunes?
Or maybe the way it creaks as it sways in the wind, the way it moves
like seaweed breathing in the tide. Is it because it can't keep anything
in or anything out? Or is it because, despite all that, it's found
the strength in the slant, the speck of stillness that hides
itself somewhere on the point of collapse? I think I know –
but I wish I didn't, so I'll make the turn as fast as I can, so fast
you'll only just see me do it. It reminds me of you
in that white room, taking too long to die, stopping
and starting, huffing and puffing your way to the door,
dragging your great ribs into the leaves like an old bear.

NED DENNY

The poems gathered here span approximately thirteen years, the earliest ('Tree') written whilst living in a cottage in the foothills of the Himalayas and awaiting the birth of our son. Almost half of them were written over a decade later in another cedared idyll – the Duke of Bedford's former estate on the banks of the Tamar, where Devon ends; both troubadour adaptations date from this latter period, 'Who's She' having been entered for the 2015 Spender Prize along with the following commentary:

> I didn't set out to translate Arnaut Daniel, being somewhat awed by Ezra Pound's versions of his robust and adroitly patterned songs. Master of the elaborate, allusive style known as the trobar clus and inventor of the sestina, Daniel is the poet referred to in Dante's Purgatorio as 'il miglior fabbro' ('the better craftsman', the term later used by Eliot – dedicating The Waste Land – of Pound himself). My unintended remake of 'Doutz braitz e critz' began with the gift of the first line, a lucid four-syllable seed and slight departure from the Old Occitan which is usually rendered as something like 'sweet trills and cries'. This then grew in line 2 to declare the apparent paradox of something both highly ordered and numinous, condensed yet expansive, Apollo and Dionysus in one ('mind-manifesting' being the literal meaning of psychiatrist Humphry Osmond's 1950s neologism 'psychedelic').
>
> After the minor liberties of this opening my concern was to echo and renew, in a language less rich in rhymes, the shape and light of Daniel's original: the stanzas consisting of seventy-five syllables in regular array, and chiming with or calling out to each other like island universes or groups of birds in different trees. It felt like an affirmation of my initial instinct to read, several weeks later, Pound's contention that 'precision of statement' is what Daniel can teach. As for the unnamed 'she' of my title, the proverbial cat's mother, it will perhaps suffice to say that the troubadours were her wise and foolish warrior-devotees. Now as then, it is at the same time a question you might ask in a noisy, crowded room and one that lets us approach the mystery and radiance of our origin.

I like to think that my own sestina 'Drones', despite being set in a modern-day UFO conference, wouldn't be entirely alien to Daniel and his kind. Long live the *trobar clus*...

Untitled

after Baudelaire

I have not forgotten that bone-white house
where town succumbs to countryside,
the lopped statues of Love and Abundance
loitering in baroque undergrowth,
and, near dusk, the tide of the sun,

which, seen through windows streaked with clouds,
resembles an omniscient eye
observing our nuptial feast in silence,
casting the long gaze of its glow
on the empty plates, the torn net curtain.

Old Song

Observe the elusive nature of the goddess:
she is nowhere to be seen in your languages,
but on your vision's periphery, the garden's
every leaf is exultant with her presence.

To Catch a Thief

You've been dead a generation and yet there you are still,
poised and serene and scarcely more than twenty,
divine, unattainable.

Incomparable Grace, you marry a prince and grow old.
When I ride in pursuit of the enemy,
though, it's your face on my shield.

Fir

after Bernart de Ventadorn

When you see the sun-made lark's wings whirr
against the counterpressure of that light
and slow until a hypersonic stillness
has him drop, a stone shaped like a heart,
it's as though you step into a green rain
of envy of those whose smile is no disguise,
marvelling that your chest's flagrance
isn't instantly reduced to a spent black wick.

You thought you got love but your thoughts were
simulacra, a counterfeit delight,
for what idea can cage the pace of the kiss
you pursue in dreams and trace in art;
she has stolen your blood's loving refrain,
nabbed her sweet self, has purloined the very skies
and in so doing's left a dunce
caressing thin air to the soundtrack of a tick.

You're no longer the fat controller
of yourself, squinting from a tourist's height,
since you glanced into those eyes where all joy is;
as mirrors hold death and life apart
they disclosed your second self, free of pain
as a meat suit is nipped at by shoals of sighs;
you're shut out from your days, as once
Narcissus was undone by his own biopic.

You'd wash your hands of her and all her
kind – whose ways are at ease, whose touch is light –
vowing that just as you once sang her wholeness
now your branching tongue shall flick and dart,
seeing how they close their ranks and disdain

to aid one who shakes in her dawn air, who dies
into the vast clairaudience
in which each open tree receives an old magic.

And in such things, alight under fur,
she shows herself to be a girl alright,
not resting content with the bland park that is
permitted by that celestial fart
but reaching for the fruit that fires the brain;
I'm afraid that you're a joke in her bright eyes,
roped to the cliff of appetence
with no companion but the music of your pick.

Grace is gone from the world, you aver,
yet what have you ever known but this night
in which the sainted mother of our riches
has been replaced by a doll, a tart,
a bulb-eyed changeling whose synthetic reign
is the false light, a grim tree, which if you're wise
enough to unspell appearance –
now's the time – you'll know for the shade that makes us sick.

Your tame prayer is just a verbal blur
wholly failing to manifest your 'right'
to her who can be the riskiest mistress –
the cyclone her voice – so why not start
a trilled silence, burn books, begin again;
let death be the force that you ventriloquise,
that end which is the newborn dance
danced in exile by those who are so slain they're quick.

House Music

Consider the architecture of the fire,
this radiant palace receiving in turn
the great bare mouth of the smallest creature
and the mirrored, steel-cored tower
of your pride; consider that soon
that grim ember

resembling the face we all fear or desire
will be the perch where you sing and do not burn,
peace be within thee, vigilant preacher
of the mind-consuming hour
each undergoes and what the moon
must dismember;

and consider while these agile days climb higher,
witchlike as flame – as the stuttering intern
is fanned to a tall and brilliant teacher –
how to step into that power,
that breathing room, the killer tune
you'll remember.

Cutting Class

We slip by the brick estates
patterned like a lizard's back,

then suburbs where the conifer's
black flames stand sentinel;

we pass the clipped, uncanny gardens,
pace through the witchcraft

of the giant leaves of planes,
wade against the smoking tide

of insect-faced and swollen cars.
We skirt the sewage works,

cross over the motorway's grey
cortege to the dark

matter of the countryside –
Egypt's pylons scanning the fields,

evil spores in the undergrowth,
antennae needling the clouds –

and we just keep on toiling away
from town, setting our sights

on the grace and madness
of burning trees, as far as where

the truant woods dance
in a light that is breaking all the rules,

to the point at which we start to learn
to stand inside the fire.

Drones

You see the Greys, he said, girding his teeth
for a lime doughnut, they use the owl's
nervous system the way we use a drone
or hidden camera. Given what I now knew,
it almost seemed possible. When green tea
was announced I slid outside for a smoke,

paced roided grass, watched where stained smokestacks smoked
into the wind's dead breath, its yellow teeth.
Back in the conference centre, the tea-
fresh crowd were pondering the giant owl
that stilled her car on that night when she knew
she knew nothing, its voice a savage drone

terrible to recall, a rising drone
which turned her body into pixel-smoke
swarming upwards and assembled anew
('like I'd been sucked into a white hole's teeth')
on that craft that swept as quiet as an owl.
When she arrived home, hours late for tea,

her forehead was marked with a tau cross: T.
She paused, and the air conditioning's drone
momentarily quickened the cased owl
on the wall, living eyes long gone to smoke,
and shivered through the symmetrical teeth
of love's lost children (tell us something new!)

who'd come here to share what little they knew.
I thought of the onset of DMT –
that sense of deliverance into the teeth
of a buzzing gleam or luminous drone,

mere seconds after releasing the smoke –
and then of that line from Twin Peaks, 'the owls

are not what they seem'. I dozed, dreamt of owls
sane and inviolate in all they knew,
and awoke to the guest lecturer: *Smoke
And Mirrors, Carl Jung and the Abductee.*
With his grey skin, dark clothes and soothing drone
he might have been a priest. I licked furred teeth

clean of dough, grabbed a smoke with my teeth
and headed to where I knew mowers droned.
Love is an owl and it's having you for tea.

Era

I bought it because of the backwards 'S' and the teeth
of the mouth, the jagged lip: DADDIES FAVOURITE
ƧAUCE. He unearthed it in the seventies. It cost me
a pound or a fiver. 'An error. Unusual. "Under the
radar".' His wink made me think of the interloper,
of things renewed, of things reversed. The glass was
the clearest, palest blue.
                    When I handed it over, a bird
called from the garden – this is just as it happened,
I have it here – and you read it as DAD DIES. That
made me cry. That made me wonder.

Who's She

after Arnaut Daniel

Sweet precision
of the mind-manifesting
voice of the birds, the luminous argot
blown from tree to tree just as we implore
those whom love makes us see more and less clearly,
you inspire me – whose perverted soul sways true,
straight in its windings – to conceive the finest
call, a chirp with no bum note or word astray.

Indecision,
that luxury! No dithering
could touch me when I first breached the snow
of her smooth ramparts, the girl I thirst for
with a wild intensity that is nearly
unendurable, the shining one, she who
has hands whose omniscience exceeds the rest
as surely as love's gentlest caress bests a

circumcision.
She clocked me, my discerning
between the real deal and the fake – *we* know
how true gold's hidden by the lead uproar
of our toys – and as our tongues moved sincerely
she drew her dark cloak of constelled blue
so the boys that speak in the snake's interest
couldn't leer at what all babble fails to say.

No spring vision
(birds interpret as they sing)
of flowers limning the unguarded flow
of heaven is fresher; without her, *L'Or*
gives skin no glow nor JPMorgan's yearly

profits; within her high castle's living pew
our seeming leaders might be less possessed,
all who exchange her presence for the Devil's pay.

God's elision
in life's book of our killing –
that only sin – our joy with our sorrow
surely bodes well for his setting some store
by holy communion, wherein we'll merely
look and kiss and laugh along each bared sinew
as I measure the lovely weight of a breast
where the light, the embodied light, swells its ray.

Ah, derision
for my own solemn honking
bites once more – sound in which we think we go
about the gardens of an emperor,
dreamt court in which we whisper cavalierly
as his money man – and I'd be a fool to
mouth her name and put love to the test:
no saint protects those whose chatter keeps the dawn at bay.

Tree

for Zephir, b. 18.8.04

I root myself at the heart
of lucid, pathless space,
fingers in all directions
braced against the silence.

I am a pine, bristling
with dark electricity.
For a hundred million years
I have brooded over mysteries.

I am a plane, my great leaves
flapping like anoraks
beneath the cocksure
patter of the rain.

I reach from dirt to light,
equally expansive
in skies and under earth,
basking in blackness

and gripping empty air;
I am a splintered column
taking heaven's weight,
a river falling sunwards,

a mind lit by strange birds
at the heart of space,
fingers in all directions
opened to the day's clear flame.

SUMITA CHAKRABORTY

In the summer of 2014, my younger sister suddenly died at the age of twenty-four. The cause of her death remains undetermined. Her death became the main interest of this poem, which takes its title from the English-language translation of *Priya*, her Sanskrit-origin name, and on which I worked for the subsequent two years.

While the poem is therefore an elegy of a kind, it was my hope to write the mood of elegy rather than an elegy proper, or to write a way of inhabiting grief rather than exactly writing about grief. As a result, neither its subject nor its addressees are my sister alone, and its references range widely, including Louise Bourgeois, Nina Simone, Calvino, *Beowulf*, the names of horses I once saw at the only horse-riding competition I've ever witnessed, and more. As that list as well as the length of time I spent writing this poem might indicate, several different texts and interlocutors were on my mind as I wrote it. Four repeated touchstones were: *Paradise Lost*, to which I listened on audio-book often during those two years; Brigit Pegeen Kelly's *Song*; Alice Oswald's *Memorial*; and Marie Howe's *The Kingdom of Ordinary Time*. Howe's title is the phrase that often comes to mind for me when asked to describe this poem. The mood of elegy, I found, is diverse and capacious, containing bliss and misery alike; inhabiting grief happens in the day-to-day procession of the most ordinary time, which can also feel like a kingdom – one that is at once evil, or blighted, and beautiful, not to mention everything in between. These decisions motivated each aspect of the poem, including its syntax, form, and diction. The desire to write the mood of elegy or to write the experience of inhabiting grief became, as such, not dissimilar from what I tend to hope of any poem or tend to admire in poetry: that it will write into being a world that already in some way exists.

Dear, beloved

Child. We are done for
in the most remarkable ways.
– Brigit Pegeen Kelly, 'Dead Doe'

It would be winter, with a thin snow. An aged sunbeam
would fall on me, then on a nearby summit, until a mass
of ice would come upon me like a crown of master diamonds
in shades of gold and pink. The base of the mountains
would be still in darkness. The snow would melt,
making the mountain uglier. The ice would undertake
a journey toward dying. My iliacus, from which orchids bloom,
would learn to take an infant's shape, some premature creature
weaned too soon. My femoral nerve, from which lichen grows
in many shades, would learn to take breaths of its own
and would issue a moan so laboured it could have issued
from two women carrying a full-length wooden casket, with dirt
made from a girl inside. The dirt would have been buried
with all of the girl's celestial possessions. Bearing the casket
would demand more muscles than earthbound horses have.
The girl would have been twenty-four. This was my *visio*.
Sometimes I think of it as prophecy. Other times, history.
For years it was akin to some specific land, with a vessel
that would come for me, able to cross land, sea, the spaces
of the universe, able to burrow deep into the ground.
Anything could summon it – a breaking in cloud cover,
wind chimes catching salt outside my mother's window,
a corner of a painting. And I learned how to call it, too.
This is the only skill of which I have ever been proud.
When my sister died, from the head of my *visio* came offspring
in the thousands, armed to the teeth, each its own vessel.
My first, their mother, lived on. For itself and its hoard
it found a permanent home in a cave at the bottom of a lake.
And it waited until I was standing on a mountain to sing to me:

You will call this mountain home until I tell you to move again.
There will always be more of it underground than you
will ever see with your eye. And so it turned out to be true.
And so when I stood on the mountain that became my home,
I beheld a dirt sea, and saw our moon, which has two faces.
I learned that one face of our moon is dappled with maria,
and that the sunbeams here are newborns that lie
on each other, purpling into the fog and outstretched pines.
The Earth spins masses of air until it looks like one of many
irises studding our galaxy. From space, parts of the Atlantic
look like leather, wrinkled and dark, and others look
like iridescent fishes in an old Master's painting of the sky.
I live in the valley of a crater here, where steam rises like ghosts
in the summer heat. This mountain is made of igneous stone.
Every day I issue a warning to lovers: darlings, I have
in my possession a dead girl deer. Her head is draped
over my right shoulder. I hold her with one arm
encircling her torso. You wake each morning with flowers
shrouding your body, like a corpse; I put them there.
To me, you died when my legs curved around your head.
One of the deer's eyes has blackened, and her tongue is thick.
She belonged to my sister. O my sister, you were twenty-four.
Listen close. Even to this part. Especially this.
I want you to hear what I say to lovers, because I want to sing
to you, who died a virgin, a few treatises on love and sex –
how flesh and ecstasy are born, what they make,
how they live out their days. As a bodied girl
you feared me, and I met your fear with guttural disdain.
I imagine you wondered what it would take for me to hear
a mortal, human voice: whenever you spoke, a vessel came
for me, chattering like some frail and hissing bird,
pigeon-chested, thin-veined feet. Sister, I don't listen to lovers,
either, who I call by the same names that were yours:
dear, beloved. But spirits are not like their progenitors.
Their touches can range, texturally, from velvet to bristle.

Lover, each time I kiss you I name after you
a sickly feeling in my own body, as if each ailing
is a previously undiscovered moon orbiting a planet
that can only sustain the strangest of life-forms.
Sister, I know neither goodness nor mercy shall follow me
all the days of my life, as surely that I know the beasts
I inherit or create, of all unions familial or otherwise,
are speechless and brute, and bound to die soon.
Yes, there is much to love about the body.
Too, there is much to hate. I cast off care for pleasure,
and for labour, teaching my body over time that these things
can't coexist. I fear it has started to believe me.
My body has never sought wholeness the way yours did, sister.
It was always still the dull twilight of early morning with us.
You were twenty-four, and when you died, I stopped fearing
arson. When I picture us as girls, we are at the base
of the mountain from my *visio*, divining the summit
as we diminish into spots of light. We are without parentage.
On my mountaintop in midafternoons flocks of wheeling
birds gather around the crescent moon. When the moon
worms its way through the clouds, it fixes its eyes on me
and sings a song that says we live our lives chained to earth,
and that when we die the flesh falls off our bones
so our bones can turn into the driest of riverbed dirt.
Sister, when you died, your bones cast an enchantment.
We made a powder of them, and I named the powder *ash*,
because *ash* is a word with neither origin nor afterlife,
and its definition is the look a doe gets when she's been away
from her herd too long. When a person goes missing
and we don't know her name, we grant her the surname *Doe*.
With this christening we name all missing persons
part of the family of *ash*, which has no family.
Sometimes I think that each speck of *ash*
previously named *Priya* hums on quiet nights
in a frequency only the other pieces can hear.

Inaudible to the waking world she hums to herself.
That hum is how my blood became blue; in lieu of oxygen,
my body began to breathe in only the vibrations of the hum.
Blood has to be born into its colours. Or, more precisely,
it has to die into them. In Hesiod's *Theogony*, Nyx is born
of Chaos. Erebus, Gaia, and Tartarus are her siblings.
Hesiod couldn't decide whether Nyx birthed the Fates
or whether the Fates were born of someone else, but he knew
that Nyx's children, whoever they were, had no sire.
About Nyx's brothers and sisters, Hesiod writes:
Earth too, and great Oceanus, and dark Night,
the holy race of all the other deathless ones that are for ever,
and one day – what? Tell me. Tell me the song they taught you.
Tell me how you learned how beautiful Nyx is,
how you realised Zeus feared her, and how you first saw
that within her every star, from the swollen to the hollow,
from the living to the dead, is visible, powered by little
but her peerless face. When I returned north for the first time
since my father turned my sister into a powder named *ash*,
a word born of nothing and with no children, I heard her
from a seagull on the ferry I rode from the harbour to the Cape,
out of a piping plover on the dunes, in a crow's call on the highway
from Boston to Gloucester, past Folly's Cove, Prides Crossing,
Rust Island. Then, from my station again on the mountain,
I heard my own voice from a brown thrasher. That night I drove
through remains of a fresh accident on the mountain highway.
The dropping sun lit my back as if heralding fire.
A dislocated red front bumper straddled the median,
singing a song. Nyx was in the wind, and her siblings,
and they bade me sing, too, like Hesiod had asked.
Grant lovely song, celebrate the holy race of the deathless
gods who are for ever, born of Earth and starry Heaven
and gloomy Night and them that briny Sea did rear.
Soon all were singing. The median sang with the deep voice
of a woman who knows how to sing scat, and the mountain,

standing like a moon on earth, responded with a wordless song
of its own creation. Ash sang. Dirt sang. To them I lent a melody,
which is one of the things I do when I can't sleep. The secret
about lullabies: when they work, it's because they sound
like something plants would sing in Hades, on the banks
of the river dark. Oh how I wish they worked on me.
When the sculptor couldn't sleep, she drew mountains.
They were pink, red, ridged and pulsing, and rose
from valleys of blue. Or else she'd draw eyes that held
too many irises, or wombs that bore sweet cysts,
or spindle-legged women with outsized, drooping breasts,
ill-formed and misshapen eyes for nipples, uneven halos
for areolae, made of the same skin as the kind under eyes
that have been open for too long. Those songs I sing
when I can't sleep are directed to my army of *visios*.
In return, they give me images of myself as different
creatures: gibbons, a chicken with a plucked-feather neck,
an asteroid, a mountain, a volcano with the thinnest,
most translucent shell. Me, as some fantastical beast with eyes
lining the inside of my body, watching my diaphragm
turn into the ocean I saw from the ferry, watching plumes of sun
flare over it as it comes to resemble a dead animal's
long-weathered skin. Ghostly ships with dropped anchors
materialise to trawl it, and squadrons of men dismount,
searching for new blooms in terra mountainous and lush.
My heart is a sky embalmed and bright. When the phantoms
drop anchor, there to welcome their sailors are screaming pelicans
on the rocks, and parades continually wheeling of ugly vultures
in funereal garb. In their eyes, the Atlantic always looks besieged
by hurricane. *Lunar maria* means *moon seas*, but when I hear it
I picture horses, torqued female beasts who live on the moon
and whose manes are made of the roots of moon-trees.
I did not want to die, but I wanted to want death.
None of you ever knew how badly. I have practised at it.
At times I rehearsed like a dancer, surrounded by mirrored walls.

At others I moonlighted with movies set on battlefields
and abattoirs, pausing and rewinding until I could mimic
the motions of actresses who succumb to unexpected poison,
or shove knives into their bellies, or fall like Brueghel's boy.
I pretended I was standing in a castle dressed like a samurai,
looking through a barred window, knowing the trees
approaching held a promise so annihilative my flesh
would have no choice but to accept. I pictured jumping
from the top of the mountain and I sang *Love it Love it Love it*.
On my mountain the birds shroud the pines, and the pines
make a spectral outline against the valley of Nyx's body.
One afternoon here a man said to his son: *All this has to do*
with eons of time, water over and over, just cutting and cutting
the rock. From where I stand on its summit, I can touch
the Big Dipper and I can see its children, and another peak,
shaped like the back of a horse. It is shadow blue, the same blue
as the dying sky. To the Big Dipper and her children I sing a song
that asks if they are safe, and tells them that on forest floors,
dappled things of glass and light grow from knotted roots.
Sister, could I find you on that horse mountain? I wonder
if I want to. Have I made this world? Lover, a confession.
If I found my sister on any mountain, I would gather her
in my arms and take her from its back, singing lullabies.
Or else I'd take an arrow laced with a drug I'd made special
for her, and, standing close, push it in her unarmed
right flank. Instead of how to die, I ended up studying
how to kill. But the sculptor, she asked nothing of her dead.
Out of visions of them she made formidable metal spiders
she named *Maman, Maman, Maman. Maman Maman Maman*,
who live after the sculptor has died, have all lost children,
like my mother. Their domains are terrors – land-terrors,
water-terrors, terrors of the open sky. Their hearts are war-
grief. Terrors of trees in the joyless forest, of portent.
Sometimes in their homes are fires on floods, dire wonders.
Their children were all named *Doe*, which means that the plural

form for children of *Maman* is *deer*. For a long time I hated
the phrase *I am sorry for your loss*. I lost nothing. My sister *died*.
But *loss* is less of a euphemism than its users want;
to lose means both *to have been defeated* and *to misplace*.
Maman Maman Maman also answers to *Demeter Demeter Demeter*.
Sister, I could stop no one from taking your head,
although I promise you I fought for it, hand-to-hand
by the mouth of the bone-house. One day on my mountain,
I got to thinking about those other peaks. From a cave
underwater I heard: *Find them, like flowers strange*
and never before seen. And so it became true.
I found mountains covered in smoke-thick fogs,
and mountains that lied – those were barely hills.
And then I found them: what the mountains in my *visio*
would have looked like had it been summer in that land.
Summer brought some changes: my body had no orchids
or lichen, and the crown was not of diamonds, but the reek
of sewage, wafting over a field – a prairie almost –
from which rose tens of signal towers, all blinking red.
The base of mountains was, when I got there, still,
and in darkness. It was a sky in which every child of every star,
living or dead, could be heard humming. The peerless
face of the mountain was cragged rock, dust rock, shadow rock.
I stayed until day, to watch the birth of a sunbeam
so I could then see it age. Later in the day an immense heat
came, like another bone-house. I climbed the ridges, which turned
to coloured ringlets of cloud and ash at the slightest pressure.
Sunrise and sunset were scant minutes of shadow-play.
The prairie grass's rustle, each blade sang in a different language.
There I learned the names of four of the lunar mares:
Catfire, Osiris, Blood Oath, and Early Morning.
This is who I am. I harbour secret loves, and I do secret work.
Catfire, Osiris, Blood Oath, and Early Morning are teaching me
how to finally chart a course through time, how to carve
journeys in space: they descended from their moon to the crags,

followed me home to my moonlike mountain. Lover, my body –
you won't be able to keep up with it. Soon you'll have to leave it.
You'll have to leave me. Or else I'll leave you, because my body,
it invents definitions for the word *sadness*, like *noun, the feathers
on a bird's back*. You'll do nothing for me. On my mountain,
it's midafternoon, and the wheeling birds are landing
steadily, even though no stable ground is here to be found.
When they sing, it is a song that I, who know no prayers,
imagine to be gospel. A man comes up the mountainside
and sings along with them as he walks in circles on the rock.
Robbed, sister, was your breath. Robbed, lover, is yours, too.
Sister, I wish you could know this feeling: if sung perfectly,
pressure on each nerve cluster can make bones irrelevant, whether
those bones are living or dead, whether they are ash or dirt.
At the base of my mountain is a lake where creatures go to die.
Water slides into their spiracles and fills their tracheae.
Their tracheae stretch into bellows fit to extinguish the fires
in any volcano. When my body showed me *sadness*
and began there to outline and diagram the word,
another definition was *noun, a chorus of brass instruments,
like upward-turned mouths forged of metal*, and another was *verb,
to shake like chimes flanking a rock-hewn shore, barely alive
and almost imperceptible for a flash*. Sometimes I picture
my sister underneath one of the sculptor's spiders.
Her head barely reaches the first joint on the spider's leg,
and when she looks up, she thinks that the whole sky
is the spider's stomach. *Maman*, she says, *I am hungry.
Food. Food. I am hungry.* She runs her shrunken finger
from one tagma to another. Her stroke makes lava run faster
in all the volcanoes within the tectonic plate on which she lives,
and she, unawares, suckles at every ridge she can find.
She rests both palms flat against the metal, closes her eyes
and cries. What would the world look like with enough lava
to fill the Atlantic? I know that the earth's temperature
has risen, and I know that all of its ice will melt.

I know there will be no more purple from the sun, that the spider's
iron underside is one of the few things that, like my mother,
does not sing. At the lake today is a flock of feral cats.
Though they're in front of me, their song comes from below,
so although I can see them, I picture them swimming in a river
that separates mortals from the planet's heart. In this river floats
the phantom of a dead doe. Listen to me now, darlings:
my sister did not live long enough to see the moon
turn red, but I did, and despite those who wish otherwise,
myself included, I will see it again. *Sadness*'s fourth definition
is *conjunction, bees, forests of them, devotional and thick enough*
to knot together human dreams, or human bodies, even when ghostly,
or lovelorn. The underground river gives me no passage,
despite my dreams of the phantom that dropped anchor
somewhere, and of its amassed pelicans and vultures.
Each ghost is filled to the brim with flowers whose scents
describe the places they were born, just like mine does,
no matter how hard I try to cloak it. On the top of my mountain
a man says to a woman: *I like how there's just trees. Trees trees trees,*
she replies. Each time she says the word, her voice makes
a new species. I recently tried another way to die: could I fall
from a tower filled wall-to-wall with twenty-four thousand
living flowers, each planted in the soil covering the tower's floors,
six inches deep? The flowers would have heavy-branched
spikes for blooms, and would release a powerful smell
of bone marrow, and spew a pollen that fills the air until
it becomes oppressive. When I opened my mouth to sing
of this, instead of a sound my mouth expelled gnats and fog,
which is what a spider's milk is made of. The word Nyx
tastes like *sister* and means both *night* and *flower.* I worry
I won't rest again. Do you know how a naked Titan looks,
sister? He's swarmed with shadow, but he holds light deep
in his stomach, like an electric secret. Dear love,
I can't give you what you need from me. All I'll do is take.
After my sister died, I learned she always wanted a warm island,

SUMITA CHAKRABORTY 61

garlands draped around her neck. There was no mountain
in her vision. Instead, in it she was singing what she imagined
was an island song in a language I don't know. She was dancing
badly, and breathing with great labour on burnished sands.
Sand bores me, sister; I need rock and high altitude.
When I am cold, I hear wolves. I think they live in the carillon
beside the mountain's lake. Sister, it was always true
that I would outlive you. I know exactly how many times
my family wished me dead. *Don't look up*, says a child
on the top of my mountain. *It makes you want to fall*.
It will always be still the dull twilight of early morning with us.
This is one of the curses of living. In the end, my *visio* alone
will sing and dance, breathing heavily. Every day the sunbeams
in it turn a brighter pink. Dears. Beloveds. All of you.
Your blood is bewitched, and bade to move into places
it wasn't meant to go, steeped deeply in poisons
it can't purge. You share the look on your face
with all the others, whether deer, child, or man.
If you look deeply enough into any other pair of eyes,
your heart valves start to change allegiances. Your body's lakes
fill with the other's want, until all you want, in turn,
is what the other wants, which rises in you like seawater.
There are species of flowers and invasive weeds that live only
in another's gaze, whether lovelorn, hate-filled, hopeless,
or hungry. I am looking into your eyes right now,
and in my mind are two girl deer. Sisters. With thin-hooved
legs steady, digging into grass. They disappear into the woods,
which are part of a forest in a painting. When the novelist
saw this painting, he thought that there he could see men
turning into birds and birds turning into men,
and those same men turning then into sea creatures,
and then back into birds. From this final change
scales and tentacles would linger on their backs
as they wheeled through the air, as would the dream
of filling their lungs with the sea, for which they would ache.

The definition of *deer* is *lost*. The definition of *beloved*
is *dissolution*. On the top of my mountain I hear a mother
call to a faceless child, *Where are you?* The chattering
and thin voice of a boy from the top of a tree cries back,
In the woods. And then, beguilingly: *Come into the woods.*
Around the orbs of light in the forest that I still don't know
if the Dipper's children can see, new trees grow beside the pines:
elms, birches, willows, one strange Western juniper.
Each creature in this forest was once something, or someone, else –
the novelist was right. The top of one of the elms
is a sprig of radiant blood. Sister, I was very young
when I found out you were cloven-hooved. I did what I could.
I want to say that you can trust me, that I am listening to you,
and that you can speak to me and that I will speak to you
at last. Tell me about the beasts that got you. The beasts
who carry me when I am too weak to carry my deer alone
are Catfire, Osiris, Blood Oath, and Early Morning.
I would like to believe that I carry this deer for you,
that I'll be able to tell you what it feels like to have
a hungry mouth on your lip or nipple. I want to say:
Sister, I promise. But the definition of *myth* is *noun,*
the idea that any one creature can ever hear another.
And while I beguile you to betray yourself to me,
like lovers do in their sleep, I am lying to you. No, death
did not bring this to us. It has always been true. I, sister,
am a selfish woman, and you, sister, were a mute one.
My body invents words and swells with prophecies.
Its effort shows in insect bites and rashes that don't heal,
in my peeled hands, bleeding groin, wistful gut, misaligned jaw,
mole-like left eye, lump-riddled womb. Dears. Beloveds.
You've been asleep a long time, but we all return
to the waking world someday. And when you do at last
come back, you will find me spent and alone, ugly,
wounded, ungrateful, ill. Shaking and calling to you for aid.
Loveless. Without a soul or even the memory of pleasure.

The last lover to desert me will deem me rancid.
The last thing I hear my sister's voice from will be dirt.
Of the mares I will have left only Early Morning,
who won't know that I will soon take her hide,
turn it into an ocean that will, at last, cleave open my skull.

ANDREW WYNN OWEN

These poems are, broadly, about love of life and flexibility of perspective. 'The Mummies' Chorus' was prompted by Leopardi's 'Dialogo di Federico Ruysch e delle sue mummie'. The mummies wonder what life was and why it has been taken from them. 'The Kite' considers two different images of elation, flight and dance, concluding on the side of the latter. 'What Matters' explores some ideas about what is important in life and comes to see that even seemingly run-of-the-mill events, like sneezing, can matter very much. 'The Borderline' is quizzical: where is the dividing line between things? Often there isn't one in nature already, so humans impose one arbitrarily. 'The Ladder' is about the strange joy of sunsets, the 'fierce solace' of that calm. 'Sand Grains' finds fascination in intricacy, the fact that zooming in can bring both more and less into view. 'April Shower' is again about joy in nature, this time ecstatic. Rain, so often grumbled at, can bring a change in pressure and a sense of relief. 'The Rowboat' charts celestial and earthly concerns, the difficulty of choosing between one and the other. 'The Multiverse' is the capstone of this sequence.

With the idea of the multiverse as extended metaphor, it is a reminder of our duty to remember both happiness and sadness, not to neglect the prevalence of suffering or the real good that is in the world. Rationality missteps if it becomes reductive and emotionless: 'To notice this / Can change one's spin on life, if not the quantum spin.' The final poem, 'Till Next Time', takes its refrain 'How could it end in any other way?' from Robert Browning's 'Andrea del Sarto', a dramatic monologue by a painter whose skilful precision is not matched with human passion. This is a problem not just for artists, but for lots of people: as W. H. Auden writes, 'I learned why the learned are as despised as they are. / To discover how to be loving now / Is the reason I follow this star.' These poems are, together, a reflection on how wrong it would be to forget how to be loving. The mind is various and these are attempts to clarify the difficulties and delights that this can present.

The Kite

At last it lifts.
It leaves
The turf that had no more to offer it,
And drifts
Above the eaves
With every trace of ground-devotion quit.

Backtrack. Bounce back. Held in
By thread, simplicity on wings,
It rumples, thick and thin
Against its bones,
And structure sings
As it disowns
The fiddliness and pinionedness of Earth,
In soft rebirth.

It is a kite,
A kit
For getting airborne in pursuit of joy,
A sight
Designed to fit
By being both a triumph and a toy.

Yet flight is just one answer
To finding Earth a sapped domain.
Swivel and see! A dancer
Shimmies across
A sunny plain,
And all the loss
From time's interminable fade-to-grey
Is blown away.

The Mummies' Chorus

a long way after the Italian of Leopardi

What was that unripe bitter time called life
When we could shake our limbs
And hotfoot with the best of them?
Compressing garlic with a knife
Or singing harvest hymns,
Was all that jazz the snagging of a hem?

What were we then?
Is it too late to reach that state again?
Are armoured chariots still raced
At Karnak, where the makers traced
Blueprints to craft an automatic car
For Amun-Ra?

The sun will soar tomorrow, while we lie
In sand-nudged pyramids:
Sacred shapes that symbolise
Perfected form, which cannot die.
Below resplendent lids
Survive our carven and enduring eyes.

What Matters

What matters is the starlight on the rocks,
    The racketeering force
        Of joy,
    Irrumpent and unpent and hoarse
At every fragile kickshaw that the clocks
        Destroy.

What matters is the work we vanish in,
    The moments we can be
        Released.
    Incontrovertibility
Of being absent. Thus we re-begin,
        Re-pieced.

What matters are the days we rise to share.
    The casual way you sense
        A breeze,
    Which gathers presence, grows immense
Simply by being free within the air.
        I sneeze

This morning in the sun because it matters.
    I watch the rush-hour pass
        Through lines
    Of highrise glamour, plated glass.
A hardy marvel. Even if it shatters,
        It shines.

The Borderline

I watch the shadows spread
Like Petri-dish bacteria across
   The new-mown lawn, as sunbeams toss
   Their tawny mane and all the red
      Corona-rays immerse
   Thick light in cloud, which descants when
   Penumbra run their regimen
Of self-dissociations, and disperse.

   No borderline between
The pinkish heights and blood-red sun is clear.
   It is familiar but a scene
   That baffles still, where colours veer
      And coruscate around
   I can't think what. The evening sky
   Is sceptical of any ground
For saying what's divisible, or why.

   And maybe all our task
(Or much of it) is differentiation.
   The world comes integrated. Ask
   That oak, which with slow concentration
      Collects a crown of air
   And angles for the windy light.
   To be surviving is to care
For joins and ruptures. Evening, day and night.

   No nuance that I know
Can capture all the subtleties of light.
   It is the most effusive show
   World-fabric has: sun's dynamite,
      Which loves us. Is requited.
   As shadows pass and leave no sign

Of passing, so I stand, delighted,
And watch these borders of the borderline.

The Puppet

Some days I look above my head and see
A hand that flexes, jumps, and, startled, vanishes.
            Its partings leave
        A sense of vacancy,
As if to say, 'The sort of mind that banishes
            Its puppeteer
            Begins to veer
                Too near
                The wind.'
            As if that hand,
Now ravelled in unseeable blank sleeve,
    Had been the plotting force that pinned
My life in place and made it go as planned.

That's what I guess but, soon enough, this goes
When, glancing down, I spot organic links
            Clasping my feet
        And grass about my toes,
Green Earth's effusive countenance, which thinks
            It knows my mind
            And, sure, I find
                Its twined
                Support
            And givingness
A gentle guidance, patterned and complete.
    I realise that the hand I thought
Was besting me had only meant to bless.

The Ladder

It is the hour when come-and-go
Carouse around the riverbank,
   Collect in wish and wing,
     And tickle blank
Expanses of the woodland dank.
Light descants on the fields I know
   And makes their outline sing
     An interplay
     Of night and day.
Ivy and trellis, cloud-encumbered light
Conglomerates, then mottles out of sight.

   Fierce solace. Loom. Release. Good loss.
     A mumble. Mellowness?
No words. A luge within a larger way
     I thought I'd lost. Did not
We all? It turns and is a stay,
Convening marvels known and not.

   Loosed, these impressionistic phrases,
Because, alone, I am at last
   Released from hectic talk,
     Resolved to cast
The shaky scaffold of what's past
Outward, away, and watch the phases
   Of fascination walk
     Under the eaves
     Of stars and leaves
As sunset's ladder tumbles through the sky:
Soleil couchant with rungs of purple dye.

Despondency turns daring love.
　　　Reluctancy turns lift.
Sight turns ekstasis. Stand-still turns to play.
　　　All thoughts are turning, and
　　　The turns themselves turn to a stay,
　　　Unplaceable but close at hand.

Sand Grains

Almost not anything at all, this particle
　　　Of disconnected shell,
　　　Yet squirrelling and shot
Through with a chutzpah fit for Frank Lloyd Wright.
　　　Sheer angled mell,
　　　A plankton's cot,
It chuckles mischief, challenging the light.
　　　A miniature motel
　　　Where some detective plot
Might stumble, after rambling, on an article

Of lace, to solve its long-pursued conundrum.
　　　Eureka. Awe. A crux
　　　Hounded between the trees
For donkey's years, corroborated. Truly,
　　　Eternal flux
　　　(Whatever wheeze
We try to pull), although it seem unruly,
　　　Yields reverence redux.
　　　As everybody sees
Sooner or later, nothing here is humdrum.

The Rowboat

I'm in two minds about the whole affair.
　　I like the forward-wading dip
Of oar descending through expectant air.
　　I like the way that wavelets tip
　　　　Across the prow,
　　　　Which rises now,
Then drops before the rippling waterline
　　Like pilgrims at a shrine.

　　　　But then I catch the sky
Meandering immeasurably over
　　　　The windy land
　　　　That trembles by
　　While ecstasy, a supernova
Discovered best when stumbled on unplanned,
　　Electrifies it with a pang
Of thrill and thought like an interrobang.

Truly, there needn't be a choice between
　　The gentle boat and tingling sky.
The one's a stand from which the other's seen,
　　And yet this restive wish to fly
　　　　Would have me sail
　　　　Above the pale
Well-gardened houses on the riverside
　　To where the swallows glide.

　　　　Impossible to break
The up-and-downing nowness of the boat.
　　　　Not on the cards
　　　　To lose the wake
　　That fans behind the place we float.
Right here, right now, is life: for all its shards

And jostling imperfections, who
Would care to speed like flung neutrinos do?

April Shower

Rainforest day! Rain's free for all.
And here I'm getting drenched
With everything the moody clouds had clenched
But now let fall
In plosive drops,
Startling the land and pulling out the stops.

Torrential fuel. A shapeless rush
Of see-through resin beads
That shatter into absence on the turf.
It is a crush
That nips and feeds
The river where the waterboatmen surf.

One day I guess my mind will slip
Softly out of my head,
And I'll be left as some I've known, sat up
At noon in bed
With fragile grip
Clutching a nearly-gone (or part-full) cup.

The rolling shutter staggers all.
A pigeon's dappled wings
Are more-dimensional seen through the rain
It does not stall
But as it flings
Against the air it doubles round again.

I can't not stare. I'm overrun
　　By smallnesses so grand.
I think of when, a kid, my mother told
　　Me how to hold
　　The rain in hand
And drink it as, she said, she once had done.

　　This is an April shower and I
　　　Am caught off-guard by joy,
Although I know that I, like it, must die.
　　　Let death deploy
　　　Its every trick.
Delight, a deluge, cuts me to the quick.

The Multiverse

In one world, it's all slides and tinkling laughter:
　　A monkey rolls you tangerines
　　And sunshine shows you what you're after,
With not a flicker. Solar-powered machines
　　　Propel new towns
　　Above the hills of Martian moons
　　　While, back on Earth, dull frowns
Transmute to sheer elation in hot air balloons.

But it's a different story in this other world:
　　　Impulsive rocks
　　Splat pioneers. The hasty flocks
Of herons push an aeroplane off course,
And in the navel of volcanoes what is curled
　　　But imminent destruction,
　　　Eruptive force
And, diametric, slow, some distant plate's subduction?

Still, in that former world, the life is lucky.
        The lovers? They are always true.
        The heroes are sincere and plucky.
    Your footsteps know, by instinct, what to do.
            For now at least,
        Warmongers reach a compromise
            And shares of land are pieced
Between free shepherds who rejoice below clear skies.

But elsewhere God or restless mathematics meant
            To fix it so
        That days are short and passions go.
    We can't imagine what the reason is.
It chances that, for all our intricate intent,
            We stall where we begin.
            To notice this
Can change one's spin on life, if not the quantum spin.

Ants, Spiders, Bees

The ants are those who seek the bric-a-brac
                              Of evidence
And run it through the ringer, forth and back,
                              In search of sense.
Ants like to gather reams of information
                              And neatly fence
These finds in careful graphs of their creation.
                              With scatter plots,
Venn diagrams, and Power Point presentation,
                              They call the shots
On showing solid things that are the case,
                              And also what's
Improbable, or would be out of place
                              Amidst their stack
Of knowledge, which they work so hard to trace.

Contrariwise, the spiders spin their minds
                              In planned designs,
Inventing miracles of many kinds
                              With tiny twines
Which gradually accumulate to make
                              A land of lines.
They never tire, or ever take a break
                              From making maps.
It seems a thankless task they undertake
                              And yet perhaps
Sunlight on morning dew may lure some klutz
                              To try their traps
And thereby wriggle from the usual ruts.
                              Yes, yes, it binds,
But it releases! And that must take guts.

The bees elect to forge a middle course.
                              Fierce wanderlust
Wings them to anthers, pollen towers: the source
                              Of precious dust,
Which they convert to deck their citadels
                              With waxy crust.
Hexagonal, their labyrinth of cells
                              Encloses sweet
Effusions, while sheer industry impels
                              A moving feat:
The manufacture of topography,
                              On which they meet,
Enjoy their lives and, daily, by degree,
                              Must reinforce.
It is a brilliant thing to be, a bee.

Till Next Time

How could it end in any other way?
Pastels above and tangled grass about our feet,
  Tangential streaks of iridescent grey,
Highrise conjectures on invention's scope, and wheat
        Accumulating, hushed,
        By B-roads where a rushed
  Commuter hurtles to another day.

  Remote, flamingo-gawky, cranes release
Piratic hooks like pensive anglers at a river,
  Expecting, wordless, some disrupted peace
To sanction free-for-all: their moment to deliver
        Mechanic justice. Who
        Could function as they do?
  Who grips the nettle, grasps the golden fleece?

  Time past lies like a hogshead on a tray.
Fresh salmon surge upstream. Downstream young lions leap.
  Time's yes-man has relinquished yesterday.
All doubts disintegrate. Enthusiasms seep
        And gather. Where they flow,
        Life flourishes. Trees grow.
  How could it end in any other way?

ZOHAR ATKINS

I wrote these poems over a seven-year period, while pursuing a doctorate in Theology at Oxford and rabbinic ordination in New York and Jerusalem. For me, poetry is the discipline of subverting discipline; it is theory in reverse. Or as Heidegger put it, 'the thinker says what being is; the poet names what is holy'. As a scholar, my task is to analyse, demystify, explain. As a poet, however, I am summoned to confront what courts analysis only to flout it. My task is to let the mysteries I encounter in daily life reveal themselves as yet more mysterious than I could have presumed.

Poetry is my argument with myself. But it is also my argument with argument. In following its leads, I hope to arrive at a clearing where the words that brought me there seem both trivial and providential, utterly contingent and omnisignificant.

Protest

No sooner do I say
'Let there be light'
Then a horde of angels arrives
With their signs.

'No more oppression of darkness!'
'Stop occupying our empty wild.'
'Down with the visible!'
'God Should Know Better Than to Speak.'

Even the walls of my hotel lobby seem
To sing out against me.
But then I remember, I'm God.
Soon the angels will want to go home.

In the end, nobody will remember how they
Held hands, soaring together, like a school
Into the tear-dusk firmament.
How they laid their celestial torsos down in a row

To prove my world a desecration.
Nobody will hear their words of lament,
'Holy, holy, holy,' as anything
But praise.

System Baby

I was six when I first filed for moral bankruptcy
I was ten when they told me language is inherently *classist*.
At thirteen, I started defining *kindness*
as 'making nice to those who like your favourite teams'.
At twenty, I hired a ghost to write my LinkedIn profile.
At thirty, I started radiosuctive parole therapy.
At forty-one, I began to look sideways and call it *inward*.
At eighty-six, I'm a work in progress.
Today, at 120, I'm a proud piece of gum,
who's almost forgotten the countless nights it took me,
locked in the shoe of the human mind,
to get here to tell you: don't let others humanise you.
Don't let them take away your objectivity
no matter how much they brutalise you.

Song of Myself (Apocryphal)

I am my own listserve,
advertising job and fellowship opportunities
for myself by myself to myself.

I sing of unpaid internships to my soul, O soul,
and of passing controversies on which to take sides
is to take the side of the self.

I re-post myself and forward myself
and respond to myself with emojis
for I am the screen and its anticipation,

the pleasure of being liked
and of commanding myself to like others.
For all pages are contained in my potential

for sharing, scrolling, even viewing
incognito. I sign in on myself
and log out of myself and yet remain

more than my usernames
and forgotten passwords.
For I am the great web itself

and every parody known to it
is known to me, and every troll
who devastates its comments section

is of myself. I am celebrity culture
and conspiracy theory culture –
the metastasis of meaning

that nurtures both political
gossip and culture wars,
food blogs, parenting blogs,

and cat videos. What you
shall click, I shall click,
and where you shall cut and paste

I shall be cut and paste.
Do I make myself redundant?
Very well then, I make myself

redundant. I am a paywall
(disambiguation)
I contain metadata.

Poetry TedTalk Notes

Most poetry has the same shelf life as the technology of its time.
Therefore, poetry is less about the individual poem, than about the
    brand, the update, the
plan, the package, the network, the merger, the deal.
The question isn't 'Is this a good poem?' but, 'Is it scaleable?'
A poem, like a business, should always have an exit strategy.
A poem is a platform.
You can't solve all of poetry's problems in one poem, but you can use
    it to build your
profile, make connections, plant seeds.
The poverty of poetry is an asset.
The meaning of poetry isn't liquid.
Carried interest in poetry is essentially tax-free.
Reading is a better return on investment than writing.

Without without Title

A poem that admits there is no meaning
besides the gathering of syllables
into little bouquets of desire,
placed, somewhere, between light and dust,
is said to need, as winter needs,
the beauty of visible breath. If
wisdom is not to be had, it is
to be sung. A poem is nothing
but the sound of emptiness
enfleshed, or else the sound
of a half-naked emptiness
caught between an urge to strip,
a want to decorate,
and a lingering contentment
to stay here

Fake Judaism

Abraham, says Deleuze,
could only become a Jew
by first being a *goy*.

Inside every *pintele yid*
is a Pinteresting Gentile.
And inside every Gentile

is a unique ignorance
of the Midrash
that the Torah was given to everyone.

*

I have studied the yud-shaped pool of blood
like an exhausted hunter sniffing out the air for some lentils.

I have adorned myself with Bilaam's staff infection, and the lines
    on my face
record the litany of psalms I have struggled
to compose
lisping, tongue-numb from the frost of imagined taiga.

But never could I hear
the night-ram bleating out
Zohar, Zohar.

*

I've heard Bialik forbade himself from writing as a kind of sign-prophecy.
A desperate gesture towards the emptiness of his devotional rebellion.

The way Hosea names his daughter 'Ee-Ruchama', meaning there is no
    mercy,

to demonstrate that God, too, will have no mercy on his children.

The poet's silence is an almond-shaped abandonment.

Holiness, an incorrect password
to a door that has no lock, no gatekeeper.

*

To be a Jew is to pervert metaphysics
so that what matters is not ideas
about the thing or the thing itself

but the voice, departing into blessing.
A piece of fruit, embezzled from paradise
by speech alone. By speech, alone.

Déjà Vu

Tell me the absence of helicopters, there
In winter blue, above the bridge, isn't

Significant – that the upside-down sign
Advertising a world at No Additional Fees

Isn't meant to draw us into it.
And poems, tell me the years don't spread,

Vainly forming a notion
Of self-worth and haggling over the boundary

Between voice and desire. Tell me this need
To hibernate is language's way of teasing

Forth from refusal. Tell me this staff, this rock
This comma, projected into bread and blessing

Doesn't tell us everything we need to know to morph
To ward to throw unknowable music: Fire, child of snow

And snow, child of gaze. Whose? Yes. That's the point,
O chaos. So may the target of our senses and the backlog

Of our failures be constitutive of our lives that we may live
Beyond allure. Let those orange suede boots traipsing across

Your poem not dissolve your knowledge that you manifested
From a rat's periphery. She wants to be a co-author with you,

As if you were the same as you. As if the you deciding which
Words deserve to arrive – here – were not an effect of the words

They only seem to chaperone. Tell me a truth that doesn't
Reference Heidegger, a love whose knowledge exceeds all scope.

Pirkei Avot

My father used to say:

Reader and writer are like two fugitives
Examining the shade of an egg.

But my mother would always counter, *an olive.*

Now, my children taunt me:

For what did they examine?
A place to rest? A secret measure?

The ward in which they question me
Becomes a palace I can almost see.

I strain towards the meagre light
In search of something to say.

Look! The light is the size of an egg!
No, they reply. *An olive!*

The Binding of Isaac

Twenty minutes away, a young Muslim is dying of bone cancer
In an Israeli hospital. His sister refuses to donate her marrow
And the young man cries out in darkness, 'Allah, Merciful One, I know
You are punishing me for all those naked women I visited.'
And under his rage is the sadness of tank-ploughed olive groves.
We read about it in our seminar and debate the pros and cons
Of hugging him. We refer to human touch as an intervention.
'Who are you to love me?' we hear our fantasies shout back at us.
And so it was that Abraham, having heard the angel's voice
And felt her tears, untied his only son, saying, 'God has provided
The offering for us.' But Ishmael insisted Avraham had heard wrong
And said, 'My place is here, on the altar.' And Abraham said, 'Isaac, Isaac.'
And Ishmael said, '*Hineini.*'

RACHEL MANN

Must priests write religious poetry? It's a question I've wrestled with repeatedly in relation to my own writing. I am fascinated by the question's imperative: does the 'must' here mean 'necessary' or 'inevitable'? Or even 'doomed'? Is it necessary or inevitable for a priest-poet to be tied to the interrogation of the Divine? Certainly the origins of many of my poems lie in a recognition that I write in what Les Murray has called 'the new, chastened, unenforcing age of faith'. The genesis of my poems in this selection lie, in large measure, in acknowledgement of the ever-failing grip the Word has on a culture once saturated by it. I hope, however, I am not simply responding to a twenty-first-century version of Arnold's 'Sea of Faith'. Faith is all very well, but the Word is more interesting.

Perhaps the slipperiness of the Word has an analogue in the seeming frictionless quality of words themselves. One doesn't need to be a doomy Victorian or a playful post-modern to recognise the refrain that words are inadequate to speak the world. At their most basic, these poems are interested in what might be made with words when some degree of formal and rhythmic friction is applied to them.

David Jones reminds us that one of the implications of the Latin root for 'religious', *religio*, is 'ligament' or connective tissue. Ligament is a binding which supports an organ; similarly, the religious may be read as a binding or a securing which makes a certain kind of freedom possible. As Jones suggests, 'cut the ligament and there is atrophy'.

The religious binding tissue in my poems is not so much my faith, still less 'God', but my Anglican formation in the Book of Common Prayer and the King James Bible. Those texts provide the bindings for my language-wrangling. I hope, then, that my poems are not simply playful riffs on archaic phrases and gestures, but represent an attempt at what Evan Boland calls 'a forceful engagement between a life and a language.'

Dietrich Bonhoeffer, whilst imprisoned by the Nazi Regime, wrote 'There are things more important than self-knowledge.' Christian Wiman has gone so far as to suggest that 'an artist who believes this is an artist of faith, even if faith contains no god'.* If these poems say something, anything, they do so by their relative disinterest in 'self-knowledge' and their commitment to interrogating the connective tissue between words and the traditions which have shaped them.

* Christian Wiman, 'God's Truth in Life', *Poetry Review* 98 (2008).

A Kingdom of Love

I return from the garden of remembrance,
I wash the dead from my hands,
I sing the versicles for Evensong, O Lord,
My larynx trembles with mucus and awe.

Collect for Purity

I try to form prayer's capital word
On my tongue. O sweet imagination
Give it shape enough! *Love!*

Love should taste of something,
The sea, I think, brined and unsteady,
Of scale and deep and all we crawled out from.

Of first day, the Spirit's debut,
The frantic dove torn apart,
Her feathers ash on Eden.

Yet of that of which we cannot speak
We must pass over in silence –
Selah!

The Spirit itself maketh intercession for us
With groanings
Which cannot be uttered.

Fides Quaerens

Am I required to believe
In the uncorruption of saints,
The Mother's timeless womb?

There is limit, even if limit
Is never drawn. (I cannot
Give an instance of every rule.)

I don't know what 'believe in' means
In the vast majority of cases,
Which is to say I think it enough

To acknowledge the glamour of words –
Relic, body, bone – I think
Mystery is laid in syllables, syntax,

Miracle a kind of grammar,
Milk to train the tongue.

The Ordinal

I've lived for the feelings of others,
That's a listening of sorts,

What have I learned? That self
Is bitumen, black as tar,

Oh, how slowly we flow, oh
How slowly we flow, we crack with age.

I've lived for the feelings of others,
A philosophy of sorts. I've heard

Self give up its final word,
Coughs and whispers in

Hospitals and nursing homes.
Oh, how slowly we flow, oh.

The Book of Genesis

Before holy or righteous, before the Law,
Before sound was distilled into *bet, aleph, niqqud*
(So many crossings-out), before all that: Song.

Oh, to taste fricatives – damp from lip and palate –
Dental trills, the Spirit chewed by teeth,
Ejected from lungs, an offering!

Oh, to know before, before, before the Book: Decision.
Should the Apple be plucked or crushed?
And, love, what place love?

Compline

Why should I not have lovers too?
Which is to say, when no one else
Comes near, God will have to do.

Prayer is the body's work, *is*,
I was taught to steeple my fingers
As a child, form a spire, *Like this!*

Prayer ascends, it is naked, *shiver.*
O *God, avert thine eyes!* Thine eyes
Are multitude, thy tongue is bitter.

The Apocalypse of John

I.

We gather at church door
For a body, and perhaps
This is creak of Last Day,

Ten of us, eyes downcast,
Behold! A universe in pavement cracks;

I hold a Word in my hands – *Eleison* –
I whisper, In *God, nothing is ever truly lost,*
But already a Seal

Is broken and I am sick
Of rain and storm, and pale horse,

And pale horse comes to my door
And perhaps this is the Last Day,
And rain, and rain, and angels

Silent in Heaven, and dare I believe
In God, nothing is ever truly lost?

II.

A body dies and I sing Requiem,
Man hath but a short time to live,
Man hath but the validity of material things!

Requiem is black universe,
Word is gravity,
Body is praise!

III.

Yet to find one's final form,
Surely that's the meaning

Of *spes contra spem?*
The ashes of a neighbour wait

In my study for burial in a garden
Of grit and peonies and loam,

Soon to be carried a final time,
Soon to be earthbound,

A statement in ontology.
Ecstatic. Cool. Unravelled.

Chaucer on Eccles New Road

*'Canterbury Gardens comprises a hundred stylish apartments
for the modern city-dweller...' – Estate agent's leaflet*

From between the lines – yellow, white, stained –
speak, Theseus, speak. Of the great chain of love,
kyndely enclyning. Breathe and speak, worthy knyght.

Requite, dronke Robyn, or *stynt thy clappe.*
Traffic has a language of its own:
whispers and sighs, the chime of speeding steel,

and prying's no sin. Inquire of tram tracks,
of *Goddes pryvetee,* how long it takes to lay.
Gras tyme is doon; my fodder is now forage;

A plea for peace, Oswald reve, but here's truth:
Til we be roten, kan we nat be rype.
We all become earth, but mortar and brick?

The Pardoner is a court, prefab walls,
Ycrammed ful of cloutes and of bones,
carpet and paint. Shopping malls are relics

swarmed with pilgrims. Your garden, Theseus,
is poison. Enclyne your roof, shelter me.
Til it be roten in mullok or in stree.

Reading Ovid on the Underground

Look, Niobe comes... as beautiful as anger will let her be.

Mansion House, Monument, Cannon Street, Bank,
the electric underworld: carriages of wrists,
elbows, ripe armpits. *Stand clear of the doors.*
Words curve on all the walls. *Last chance to see!*
Five Stars, A Triumph! Pin-up faces peel.
Lear stares, his girls. He waits our flattery.

No phases of the moon for us. No sun
to mark the days. It's all show: white light, glare.
At the edge of electrocution
corpse boys, corpse girls walk the tunnels
and halls: stale breath, bodies out of time,
they teach me the meaning of words:

frantic, fears, daughters, sons, tears, alone, gone.
St Pancras, Angel, Old Street, Moorgate. Bank.
St Pancras, do you ever hear our prayers?
Our prayers are escalators. *Scala*
sounds so classy, *elevating*, but handrails
are loops of black. Vinyl prayers spin on.

Covent Garden, Piccadilly, Leicester Square.
As far down as this world goes, I go down.
Staircases move up, topple out of sight,
metal waterfalls, but no one believes my tears.
It's theatre-land. Everyone a busker here.
Michelle, ma belle. Dry your tears, I seh.

East. East. All gods arise in the east.
East Acton. East Finchley. East Cote. East Ham.
Back to the source, through the burial grounds

the Navvies bored, back beyond the dead.
Heaven's the top of a stair.
Hell's a blur, hot wind, an empty platform.

The Priest Finds Eve in Piccadilly Gardens

Mamucium: breast-place, mother, Eve –
Oh bone of my flesh, flesh of my bone,
Clay and water dredged, sweet Daub Hole.

Tonight the mysteries of glaciers
Spend themselves on tarmac. Ice-caps soak us.
We're the damp-arsed. Your favoured kids.

So this is what it's like to be cast out –
East of Eden, East of Salford, benched
With drunks. Beyond the wall, buses squeal.

We're in the dark and forget the garden
Was an asylum once. Bright lights, fierce crowds
Dance along its edge. We'd leave if we could.

Mamucium: breast-place, mother, Eve –
Clay and water. Raw bone. It's what we are.
Can you hear me, Eve? Our breath is fumes.

St Elisabeth Zacharias

Come. Beyond thirst, beyond tending,
where rose petals crisp, water greens
in a vase.

Move closer. Breathe my dust, my very flesh
settling. Be dust with me. Here where
we place the things we've gathered –

the china Labradors,
the endless cats,
the *Cliff Richard* plates

Isn't this how it should be? Piling
fold on fold, letting gravity pull
on our bones, till we can resist no more?

Don't touch me. My cells ache. My skin
so thin spiders fall through.
It would be a sin to hold someone else.

Evensong

'Love is a phoenix that will revive
its own ashes' – Thomas Traherne

September, and the orchard sags with prayer:
Strip the Fruit of Sin! Reap! Reap!

Wye lifts lime, spins pools of silt at the tip
Of fields and it is late, late, late, oh priest

Hurry on! Sing, O miserable offender,
Within thy walls of stone. Hurry on,

Witness His truth:
Glory is not a word, God is, God is

Neither noun nor verb, but shears laden fields,
He reapeth where he doth not sow.

JAMIE OSBORN

I no longer look at the photographs from my year as a teacher in Namibia; they seem like false memories and I cannot work out whether it is myself or the pervasive orange light that looks more out of place. I have an impulse to delete the pictures permanently. My poems were prompted, I believe, by that impulse, or in hope of countering what often seemed a favourable blankness by at some level replicating it.

That impulse or something like it was also the main reason I took no photographs when I spent the summer of 2016 as a volunteer in the refugee camps on the Greek island of Chios. There were, of course, other reasons, some of which have informed the poems I ended up writing. Unlike the Namibian poems, which required significant reshaping (they all began as fourteen lines), the Chios poems have scarcely changed from the forms in which they came to me. For example, not a single one of the Namibian poems has kept its original opening, while in the Chios poems none of the first lines has been altered. When it came to editing, I realised, however, that the sensibility behind the poems is the same.

There were other constants: sand kept appearing in the Namibian poems, sea in the Chios ones. But my two attempts to write more conventional 'landscape' poems, set in Namibia, were failures. They lacked feeling; lacked, too, a fundamental 'otherness'.

I am no longer directly in touch with the children or the teachers from the school in Namibia; an email exchange with one of the children, initiated four years after I had left, soon petered out. I do follow my friends from Chios on social media, but have found it hard to write to them as I move with a European's privilege to yet another NGO job while they remain on the island or (most of them by now, thankfully) in camps in Germany. I doubt that either they nor my Namibian friends will ever see this book, and even if they did, I am not sure what the poems would mean to them. The names in the poems are real but do not correspond to actual people. Nevertheless, I want these poems to be for the actual people, my way of keeping in touch despite the erasures and the 'otherness'.

Did you see elephants?

On the farm, how many types of cattle
are there, how many donkeys, sheep?
Draw seven of your favourite mammals.
Which one do you see?
               'Listen, here is bush. This one is
           the kwe-voël – the boesman used to think about it,
           something – in English, go-away bird.'
At Warmquelle, they said not to stay outside.
At Chobe, lay and looked through reeds.
Twyfelfontein: rock art, huge, red hills.
Brandberg: slept among the chickens, with stars.
Yes, Cape Town, District 6; in Durban, was mugged; Johannesburg,
     felt watched.
Fish River Canyon: camped alone. Vast.
               What else did we learn?
At Uis, something you wouldn't believe.
          Go across the alphabet, draw me one for 'e'.
Always came back to the farms, school: nothing
else to see.

Namibia, August 2012 – July 2013

Caprivian

Elephant, we were calling him, Jumbo, Grass-man,
Sibukuku, Mr Oh-Okay. He was knowing it, but still
he was greeting, 'Good-uh morning, class'
and we did answer 'Good-uh morning, Sir!'
He was listening the Zambia music: when he did dance
all the children we were laughing. He was bringing
his cherri in the school and was calling her his kudu,
then he is big and happy like elephants.

He did only beat me one time: he was talking
too much – 'I'm use, I'm use' – and we were sleeping.
He made me then to write fifty times the speakings
and the tribes of Namibia.
      I did draw for him a picture of an
elephant eating grass. After, he was saying in his
language, 'thank you'.

How we are building

      This one is my house. Here is: we are
sleeping, this one is looking after
the donkey, this one is making porridge.
The bed is nice, my father's car –
Ah-ta-ta-ta, they are eating nice things!
Chips – and meat – and ice cream –
macaroni – rice – and joguit – banana – cheese –
      This one is the ostrich. See –
he is running – at – he is running fast!
                            Take, Sir –
        Sticks, lost keys, camelthorn
        pods, butter boxes, string, two left shoes: a donkey,
        bakkies, stone
            houses, treasures –
this is how we are building: *glass, and*
        jars, vaseline, broken books, Jou
      Kombuis: koerant
        – photo me –
           we hoard
leaves, or shadows, bits
of pencil, sandgrains,
marble,
    stars

Lukas

First day: smiling, he spread his arms,
danced to make us laugh.
   Twenty years, teaching:
'they do not know they are learning, mos,
we are playing!'
Two weeks in, he beat a donkey giving birth
outside the gate, threw stones at the children who watched.
                                        Later, he gripped
our hands through the fence, laughing.
         Pink eyes, blotchy skin;
breath rattled as he poured out the problems
of the San. 'I am teaching them their language.
Look –' with an empty bottle
he jabbed at the ground. 'What is it? You see?'
Staring at the marks – 'we are playing, nê?'
– he stretched, spilled on the sand to sleep.

C22 Gobabis – Otjinene

Is my father's car – they noted
every vehicle that passed, drew
Toyota, Isuzu in the sand.
            Sophia Moses raced engine's sound
along the fence, stood pointing, waited
for applause.
            Families in overloaded bakkies
stared, drunks in donkey carts
waved.
            Every month the combi was sent
for bags of sugar, paper. We timed
exactly its return.

Lorries rattled through the night,
taking livestock north, or
beer crates for the bars. A taxi,
playing *P-Square, Chop My Money,* spewed
dirty smoke.
   Hilux: belonging to Mrs Nel,
travelling home.
     The Farming Minister tooted his horn, once.
       'It's true, it's your father's car,' we'd say,
'where is he going?' They laughed,
drew maps of their games.

No landings yet

Alicia rounds the camp. 5 a.m., the call.
Voice slurred and fuming as she *buggers*
down the beach.
     At Mandamados, she reared
a boy in each hand: *Ali Reza, darling,
you're a thief.*
    Returns, the manager,
orders toilets to be dug, tables repaired,
at her command the gate is given a *fellatial* lick of paint.
  Fuck it.
Her bosom neat, smart, from her shirt-
front she pulls
a fifty-dollar note. Ali Reza,
where can you look, when she passes without so much
   as a glance, hopeful, like us?

Skala Sikaminias, Lesvos, June 2016

Distribution

Alison buys shoes. The young men,
most alone, blow kisses
as she ascends. By torchlight from the car
we form a chain, pass
bin bags rapidly, try to save
size 39, 42,
from rain and children beating on the glass.
Alison issues: *single line, up to age twenty-four
or nothing.* Chaos, of course.
Dureid is first to bend his knee, grab
Alison by the hand. She screams.
We do not know the words that pass, only
that she slams the door, severs in the hinge
a thumb. Blood, stains.
Token of undying love, his stump
pressed against the wall, as we're
escorted out in torchlight, one by one.

Souda, Chios, August 2016

Worship

They come for water. For months, if not for years,
they've queued, fragile men and women, shepherds
from the mountains and fishwives with stone bottles
and greying, chipped hands. The tiles at their feet
are worn to troughs that still reflect the sun;
above, the dome's copper, smoothed out
since dawn.
                    Why don't they kneel?
At other churches, on other islands, worshippers come
with worry beads, cross themselves forever in blue-eyed
Mary's sight. Here, they bend, stiffly,
one arm. Preserve their families in jars of salt.
Lot's wound. On the beach
they offer cures for those
who, they say, are lost.

Mytilini, Lesvos, June 2016

Ladies' chapel

The old man in the suit squats and offers reluctantly
his meal to share. Chickpeas and chicken.
I've brought clothes – his trousers are thinner
than the grey hair patching from his lips.
And a football for the children. *What do you think*,
he says, pulling the t-shirt from between his legs
and tying it round his ribs – so Nasibeh can ask *For women?* repeat
three tents hold four families here in the stink
of cooking fat and the old man's weed as he shucks
more time, sheds chicken skin,
watches the football, clattering down the stairs.

'Al-Kanisa'/Dipethe, Chios, August 2016

Forgive me

Don't trust my people. Mohammad's hands and eyes
turn to water. At the corner,
street lamps have spilled oil on his hair, his glasses,
brilliant. He flows to your arms,
a hush in your ear. *Why don't you listen to me?*
Drunk. You need him still:
to reach deeper, gasping in the cold air.
        Behind him, the club music, beating.

Chios, July 2016

What you expect

You were packing socks when the journalists
came knocking. Warm, soft wool
or its memory kept your hands from shaking.
Roll up, fold down.
They wanted your children first, then your husband,
finally you –
            laid out another blanket,
three plates, questions
skittered to you,
watching as if the camera picking up your movements
could tether the walls' billow, could recall a house
or sheepskin-lined boots, wolfish cries
and, callous, women streaming across the street.
You look towards the interpreter, who shakes her head,
as if you'd been betrayed.

Souda, Chios, August 2016

Meidjie sings

At nightfall in the lean-to,
Meidjie sings the colours.
She sings the houses, white over green.
She sings the grey and crimson crests, the lourie birds.
She sings the camelthorn's silvering leaves.
She sings the fire, she sings the clouds,
she sings the smoke, and our frightened eyes.
She sings the night, she sings the ash, she does not sing the sunrise.
She sings the hunt, she sings for sugar. She sings the bottle stores.
She sings the dead man in the road after the thunderstorm.
She sings the storybooks, the lion and the mouse,
she sings the net and the jackal's laugh.
She sings a blue sun, she sings a yellow sea,
she sings of green grass, and a face lost in grey.
She sings our questions, how long is home, she sings of flying,
she sings of sleep. We take her sleep.
We take her voice, we take her photograph.
From her we take a dream of night,
a dream of fire; for her we dream that this is everywhere,
we dream of shelter, we dream of clouds.
We dream of children, waiting in the cold.
We dream of songbirds, we dream of ash in the stars, we dream of
    little Meidjie,
– and Meidjie sings.

Gqaina Primary School, Namibia, August 2013

MARY JEAN CHAN

As a multilingual poet from Hong Kong, I have chosen to write in English, yet Chinese is always there in my work as its foil or fraternal twin, largely owing to the fact that I only speak in Cantonese or Mandarin Chinese with my parents, and my mother does not speak English. I love how Vahni Capildeo – another Carcanet and former *New Poetries* poet – depicts her relationship to language in *Measures of Expatriation*: 'Language is my home. It is alive other than in speech. It is beyond a thing to be carried with me. It is ineluctable, variegated and muscular.' As a queer poet, I have felt language's unique capacity for carrying and transforming trauma. I have experienced how an attentiveness to form – be it a sonnet or pantoum, or simply a tercet or couplet – offers a powerful means to negotiate complex emotions that arise from our lived experiences as social, political and historical beings. I hold fast to the words of Adrienne Rich, who maintained that 'lying is done with words, and also with silence'. The poems that have been selected for this anthology represent some of my attempts at speech, with the hopes of revealing and overcoming the long shadow of shame cast by internalised homophobia and racism, all the while responding to the lyric demands of poetry: the necessity of honouring each poem's inner music and cadence.

I came to poetry at the age of twenty-one out of a desperate need for language, and found reassurance in the work of poets such as Mary Oliver, who offered my young, closeted self these generous, life-saving words in her poem *Wild Geese*: 'You only have to let the soft animal of your body / love what it loves.' I have since sought to write poems that reflect the struggles of queer youth, poems about how intergenerational trauma caused by historical events such as the Cultural Revolution can threaten to unravel the soundest of minds and the most loving of familial bonds. I wish to meditate on how we might hope to heal and care for ourselves as well as those we love in the most difficult and challenging of circumstances. Ultimately, these selected poems are expressions of desire for a more compassionate world in which we might learn, in the words of Claudia Rankine, 'how to care for the injured body' so our best selves can thrive and flourish.

They Would Have All That

To sing the evening home, the lover prepares
a pot of lentil stew – her phone lighting up to
the news of love's imminent arrival, imagining

her lover's footsteps across the swollen field,
damp with longing, her lover's steady hand
gripping her smartphone to navigate towards

some notion of home, their flat an unfamiliar
place of worship, their bodies growing close
and moving apart with the regularity of heart-

beat, blood-breath. There the lover is, running to
catch a bus she knows will take her somewhere
so she can feel once again the sensation of lack –

wondering at her lover's motions throughout the flat,
how her feet must press insistently on the floor with
each step, how the orchid must have stretched itself

a few millimetres overnight, how the stew must be
whispering on the stove and the table set for dinner.
The lovers are gentler with each other now because

they have memorised each other's fears like daily
prayer: how too much salt brings back the years of
loneliness, how a warm bath may be more necessary

than a rough kiss after a day's absence of tenderness.
The lovers are gentler because they have grown too
knowledgeable to love any other way. When one asks

the other to fling her onto the bed, the lover might say:
Do you actually want me to? And the lover might reply:
No, I don't. Such asking becomes routine, almost like

walking down the aisle of a supermarket at evening,
but it is what they do best as lovers. Beyond desire
and its petty dramas, the two women will have their

tapestry of days and nights, their hands tempered by
love, clasped bodies holding their wounds at bay.

Three Sonnets
Versions from the Twenty-Four Filial Exemplars

Èrshísì Xiào or The Twenty-Four Filial Exemplars *is a classic text*
of Confucian filial piety written during the Yuan Dynasty (1260–1368), and has
been used as an example of how Chinese children should honour their parents.

HE LAY DOWN ON ICE IN SEARCH OF CARP

One of the strangest, this: how a boy mistreated
by his stepmother still tried to satisfy her cravings
for carp, sought out the frozen lake and thawed the ice with
naked flesh, brought home two pregnant ones
for a pot of soup. At eight, I learnt this fable from
my mother's lips, offered immediately to out-do this filial son,
though there was no ice to be found all across the city –
our temperate winters incapable of frost.
Years later, I wonder why my mother did not mention
hypothermia or the possibility of drowning, did not
invite me to wonder at the boy's lack
of self-respect, did not consider how his body
deserved its own morsel of warmth, how his fingers
should never have been bait.

HE FED THE MOSQUITOES WITH HIS BLOOD

Another begins with a sacrifice: a boy too poor
to afford mosquito nets offers his blood as nectar in his parents'
stead, as he sits on their bed on hot summer nights to keep
them safe from the unbearable scorch
of inflamed skin. I read this alone as a teenager,
my Chinese now oxidised as black tea, capable
of steeping in fabled warnings. Once more, I detect
how dispensable the child's body is, how right it is that he
suffers for an ideological wound, how his parents
might have slept fitfully that night, roused by their child's
cries as the mosquitoes encircled him, or perhaps
blinking back a tear while thinking how good
their boy is, how proper this bloody
business of proving one's love.

HE DRESSED UP TO AMUSE HIS PARENTS

No longer a boy, but an old man, dressed up
as a child to amuse his elderly parents, his fists
adorned with toys: a wooden stick, a piece of polished
stone. This isn't the worst fable amongst the twenty-
four, but it makes me rage, because I am now
twenty-four, no longer in need
of dolls, though my mother yearns
for my feet to shrink to the size of her
open palms, and for the rest
of me to follow. Some days I cannot be her
child again, although I pacify arguments
and tears with a playful voice
that pleases, if only to reassure her –
and to say that love
is patient, love is kind.

respite

father slept
in the living room

to spare mother
a common cold

she coughed anyway
bereft on the silent bed

unsure of which way
to turn in the dark

mother asks: *will you lie
next to me, just for tonight?*

i said i would, sliding
into my father's skin

she slips into slumber
my head resists the pillow

as I toss and turn
into daylight

Long Distance

How long a minute lasts. Neon lights make buildings shimmer like
secular revelations. Your call tears me from my past into your present.
You ran till your feet sang on the rain-dark pavement, till you out-
paced rhythm and thunder. All the dehumidifiers are on in the house.
No fireplaces. Some seas are colder than others, some bodies warmer.

I am drinking Iron-Buddha: two teabags waiting for their time to blossom. It is too Spring here for my own good; too much green in the salad bowl. Too many stories of salvation; earlier, blue beyond belief. The moon is lying on its back in my dreams. What a smile looks like. A toothbrush touches my lips. Steamed Asian sea bass for dinner, with white rice. Polar bears have black skin. Victoria Harbor was named after your Queen. How many hearts in a deck of cards shuffled across two continents? I am catching a plane again tonight, thinking about the map on your neck. *Roaming.*

an eternal &

nothing but the enlightened land   soil loosening into surf   sinking softly
the weight of hours   every second   symphonic   ocean is never elsewhere

always here   in the eternal stillness   of depths   ripples eyeing the shore
wings arching origami   out of air   you are there   a shape I have come to

know so well   your head   is a compass   your arms   slipping between
the ocean's breath   I am ready to hold   a body of sun   kiss it nine times[*]

goodnight   time is elsewhere   as silence deafens into sound   we are holding
each other   amidst the night's falling   all the stars   have plunged to earth

a glistening pier   look I say to you   *listen   watch* how we can make it through
another day   on this shore   of lifetimes   we'll have this ocean   an eternal &

* The number nine symbolises eternity in the Mandarin Chinese language, since the word
  'eternal' [久, jiu] has the same pronunciation as 'nine' [九, jiu].

Names (I)

My mother was no tiger mom –
couldn't care less that I'd failed

maths in third grade, shrugged
when I declared I was quitting

piano at the age of seven. Instead,
she'd rage about *moral behavior*,

believed in kneeling as a cure
for ailments such as disrespect.

Once, I walked into a lift without
letting the adults enter before me,

the damage already done even as
I flattened myself against the wall,

said *sorry* and held the door open
from the inside – the wrong side.

That night, I knelt and whispered
sorry with my knees, cried to show

remorse, narrowly escaped a beating.
She was hard so the world could be

soft. *I don't want you to be hit by anyone
else.* On days when my table manners or

posture irked her, she would call me *baak
ci*: Cantonese for *as stupid as a blank page.*

There were other names for the good days:
treasure shell, heart-liver, pickled carrots.

Names (II)

I am trying to talk about you without
mentioning your name, so I say: *we
went to see a film last night*, meaning

you and I, or *she treats me very well*,
as in, you love me, or *I'm going out
for Indian tonight*, implying a candle-

lit dinner for two. It isn't always easy
keeping your name sheltered from my
mother's ears, but I try and try because

it keeps me from hearing that twist and
drop of her mouth – the way I try not to
imagine her standing next to the kitchen

sink at midnight – hungry for food or love,
though I know she shall pilgrimage to that
sacred spot over and over, the way the owl

never forgets it can see its prey best in the
dark. I have now learnt to name my loves
sparingly. You know this, don't you, how

your name will never leave my mother's
lips? I want to apologise. You do know
how much I want you – us – to survive?

Notes Toward an Understanding

I.

When you said: *why didn't you warn me*
about cultural differences, I didn't know
whether you meant my mother's face all
darkened like a curtain, or the vegetables.

II.

When mother said: *the contours of her ears*
are calamitous, I momentarily reflected on
my own auditory shells – whether they too
played a part in my irrevocable queerness.

III.

When father said: *I find language to be a*
very difficult thing, I wondered if he was
apologising for his silences, how he said
nothing when mother detonated my name.

IV.

When I said: *I want to shout at all of you, but*
in which language? – my mind was tuned to
two frequencies – mother's Cantonese rage /
your soothing English, asking me to choose.

speaking in tongues

mother says: *fan1 lei4*   分離
poet says: *behave*
mother says: *seng1 sin3*   聲線
poet says: *moonbeam*
mother says: *separation of voice*
poet says: *behave, moonbeam*
mother says: *the way you ask the moon to behave is transgressive, not Chinese*
poet says: *my voice is a splinter*

Tin1 hei3   天氣
these days
I can only speak about the weather
with a tongue splitting
spitting monosyllabic *blue* or *grey*
but did you know
I've discovered a secret
that half of my words

have been kept
like a key
under a plant which my mother
waters daily
and is something that grows
those beautiful ghosts
they seem to say:
jing6 dak1 nei5   認得你

Safe Space

where the logic of hips isn't a stranglehold to the heart

where you kiss my eyelid with the windows flung open

where a sudden light in the corridor soothes like a cure

where no one wrings the air like a drawn-out expletive

where I am naked in the shadow of morning & unafraid

Sandeep Parmar wrote recently of her belief that poetry must 'rise to the collective challenge of our times, not merely be a curio of intimate experience'. I believe this too; I'm trying.

The poems in this selection were written between 2016 and 2017. Many respond or allude to other texts: I think the ongoing work of reconsidering the historical 'canon' can help to clarify the challenges of the present. In general, I don't think it is necessary for the reader to know where these references are; 'Agony in the Garden' is an exception to this rule. The poem embeds a quotation from the statement made by John Ruskin during the annulment proceedings of his marriage to Effie Gray in 1854: 'It may be thought strange that I could abstain from a woman who to most people was so attractive. But though her face was beautiful, her person was not formed to excite passion.' Later, Ruskin based the ideal of femininity presented in 1865's *Sesame and Lilies* on Rose La Touche, whom he subsequently proposed marriage to. When Ruskin and La Touche first met, in 1858, he was nearly thirty-nine years old. She was ten.

Horse whispering

Unclear: is the better freedom to be hunted or
enshrined in chalky worship? Domestication
mostly relies upon a natural horsemanship, but
still, limping, levelled, hurt and rasping, you can't
shake the memories of the farrier's hands. Love is
a possible strength in an actual weakness.

If you will insist on riding flat-backed and spine
to spine, head over tail, feet against shoulders,
eyes to the sky, heedless of the trailing trees –
when you do fall, from me expect no sympathy.

Bathsheba's Gang

Play me like one of your sad girls, and I'll turn into
potato. I'm at my best tumescent, glowing, yellow
(I already have a piano but I don't have many friends).
And all the mascara girls are on the train again,
standing in staggered unison for Audley End.

*

Absolutely accurate and absolutely dumb an umbrella
stand leans erect against the bastion of history. Unmoved,
the world turns.

*

The hard trick is to know where to crack that horny
sheath of egotism and measure with care the contents
of that jacket's inner. *Alfred is reading 'Maud' again.*
I left the room. Your capacity for volume never matters,
they will always read in you the clattered atmosphere

of silence. But as to dead men, darling, don't worry –
there have been dead men in most rooms.

*

The latest murder and the newest thing in ghosts, fill
your big glass to its brim and scrabble again through
drawerfuls of arrest warrants. It must be relaxing to
will your own feet into murthered shoes, it must be
hard to unravel the covering skeins of your own intolerable
safety. This stuff is swaddling for the yet-to-grieve,
sic volo sic jubeo, and so the reel runs on.

*

Untwinned before the pyramid, your girl's gone groping,
flailing, through the dark. Is that your daughter, clutching
the stones? Absolutely accurate and absolutely dumb, she
is happiest, or should be, when left alone. Don't listen to
the silly bitch – Nancy Sikes! a real corker! – a great man
always knows his own. All was not well, at home.

*

Wary of nothing, you end up nothing still, and years of
careful calculus providing no reprieve I say now, heel.
Paint me a picture of your happy Antigone, or I will.

Three Caskets

I.

Why can't Cordelia be mourned? Imagine
her happy in France, leaning back in her
chair and chewing the hard corner of a
new loaf, doesn't it make you feel
sad, baby? How lovely she looks in Breton
stripes, how surely pregnancy suits her.

Is the belly really lined with lead? I know
you've books and books on the subject, I
know the store you set by precedent but
can you really wonder at the cold if you
note the storm and still stride out coatless?

To let death into your life is not an act
of murder; to shake hands with future
harm can be a peace treaty. When you
marry somebody you marry an ending, too.

II.

A snail moves steady across the vine as the
light descends into October evening. To the
left of that bright brown sheen is another
shell, this time cracked into fragments stuck
fast in the slime of its former companion,
shoe-struck and decimated. Placid movement
forward is how progress is made. The men who
dream of silent women are dreaming of their
own
      dumb
          luck.

III.

I don't have daughters but I can tell why
a snail has his house to put his head in.
In Los Angeles, you can climb all the way
to the top of the mountain without realising
you'll never be this loved by anyone again.

Naming problems

Jonny – the gardener – walks with names but I can't pay
attention. Pleasure of train running suddenly clear
of the tree line (but the danger of the city is forgetting
the forest) the real danger is looking up too late to see.

Reversible consequences. Say: *which plant is
this?* and at least you're able to describe what
you're mourning / at least name old love.

Say: *what does it do?* and you're part of a problem,
or am I making too much of our old way of
communicating? Say feebly: *I like swimming.* Say:
not in pools, I mean in rivers. Say: *I mean in the sea.*

The way your body feels when it hits the water will
stop you feeling guilty for a while that you only think in
skin / that you continue to demand of loss a glossary.

Tampon panic attack

I.

Dream dissolves of lost-limbed girls in fairgrounds, is this
a quick-come fever? Search your palms on the train to
find the rash are they always this red / perhaps you just
don't look. Waking up in bloodied underwear once felt
like shame but now is gorgeous, a victory: red sheets are
like flirting. Wisteria falling rich across the house front
evasive blue sky against brickwork evasively blue (means
actually cruel) call an election, keep calling, they can't
tell bloodied bodies from clean. Toxic shock, I christen
thee, so baby call away. Flowers / not enough / sorry. If
you think I've got a fierce red mind, wait till you see my
body.

II.

Misbegotten positive reality, muffin top just another symptom
of the excluded middle. Nothing can be both; apple-bellied is
worse than small beer. Not-A is absence, which is everywhere.

III.

Always already happening somewhere, as if the way it is done
is what is done. You first have belief, which leads to the practice /
the way it is done is usually for the best. Always already leaving
without notice, it must have already happened if you want to think
about it. Flowers are soft and so vulnerable to the diversity of
interpretation / the way you do it is what actually happens
　　Remember:
it is natural to be fearful; it is necessary to be tougher than the rest.

IV.

There is a fierce grit in the genius of girls; there has
to be, they're bleeding. 'It is interesting, but I don't
love it.' What kind of charlatan says that?

The Roses of Heliogabalus

Violets and other flowers, or roses – they
fill the mouth up all the same. The pipe
sound streams clear despite the choking
sound that muffles screaming. For those
who ate, the meal was enjoyable. For those
who drowned, their breath at least was sweet.

Thin girls

waiting by the phone
for referrals, if it happened
to men / it could be happened
at cash machines. Thin girls
wait by the phone for the
plummy voice of necessary
steps / of reassurance / arm
to shoulder. They don't come.

Angiogram

Can you inherit
motherlessness?
My fat heart says
yes.

from 'Donations'

TYPE F (CAPTIVE / VOLUNTARY)

Oil and blood for the bowed grey heads, as Aeson recovers
his usefulness, oil and blood for my own inviolable sense
of propriety. Uncontaminated, pint for pint, what's the difference
between one dog and another, between dead boy and dead lamb,
except for those small miracles as blue birth becomes gentle
continuance. The only thing to do is take it as your own
indisputable property (though even in a consumption good the
former spirit lingers) but this is bad news, for the conservationist:
we will always love most what is diminishing and so as funeral
barges stream down the marshes you wake weeping in
your yellow coat, from ruptured sleep, as if these ghosts of
our own commodities cry out, like kids for milk, in the twilight.

TYPE C (FISCAL)

Do you know the heaviness of other types of feeding?
When the time comes to bolt and deliver to the diligent
hand, accomplished at dragging up, you must place the
babe in the tour's arms, and alert those diligent sisters
to the processes of abandonment. Accomplishments
(itemised) include the delicacy of the needle, include
the practice of drawing back the suck. Overproduction,
like any other disease, can be treated. The bell rings,
and that is enough.

Agony in the Garden

Why are you walking around my garden, John Ruskin, these
are Prestige Flowers and you are gnawing like the worm. Why
must pleasure be a catastrophe? I have dedicated this sleep life
to statuary I have laboured joyfully for my base wet daughters
and you and yours have no place building nations here in the
name of purified water. When will my attention span return
from the war? Desire, hooked again, there is no inverse relation
between my dislike for you and the embarrassment you cause.

She didn't want to fuck you either *her person was not formed
to excite passion* I thought there was no such thing as bad
weather? Splendid, her skin was luminous, every blood smear
every hair-like feather. When will my attention span allow me
to achieve more? Saved for the nation, her fat tongue is full
with splinters, saved for the nation she deserved, as usual, more.

John, like sesame, like lilies, you manipulate what you have never
grown. Constant though unlessoned, stoic in the face of pleasure,
may we only tread with patience the path we have been shown.

Leaky

I.

And could you swim at Lindisfarne, softening
with sunrise and never bicker? Good intentions,
still all thumb. Pray you don't waste time. I
pray nightly never to see you too held close by
wicker, I pray but all day slapdash careful to save
face. To *have been married*, I pray nightly never.

II.

There is no counsel, no closure, no opening,
just winter. 'In leaving you, I left myself' oh
bore on, Cara Helena Derelicta. You ask: *why
must all these poems sing to me?* I am trying
very much to work on my intellectual honesty.
Some cheek, I agree, to wail after a ship I
sank myself. Hard, to learn refusal is not purity.

Thank you, Emily Hall. If you hadn't contacted me – through Myspace (*that* long ago) – to ask if I was interested in writing words for a children's opera, I am not sure whether I would have written much more poetry. Before then, it had largely stopped happening. The opera didn't happen either, but I showed you some lyrics, you set them to music, and then I started to write new words meant to be sung. We wrote a song cycle about love, then one about losing and then having a baby. Although I started writing *Life Cycle* as a male-female duet, you rightly insisted it all be the woman's voice. And so I added 'The gap so small', 'Not just milk' and 'The first turn' to poems already written. The earliest, 'Stillborn', woke me in the night. I dreamed it for two friends, Jacqui and Steve, and for their daughter, Marnie. 'Amnio' arrived after a pregnancy scan for my second son. His bones glowed in cross-section. This was a brief period, before babies in the womb were visualised as 3-D putty *putti*. Some of the poems I've written since were written *as* poems – not to be sung, and so not for you. But I have kept writing about parenthood and its losses. 'Self-Reminders' was written as just that – as a parent speaking to themself. 'Awaying' is one parent speaking to another, reassuring them they still exist. More separate is 'Friday' – one of the poems that come along in an anti-lyrical way, although I'm mostly (as you've made me) that strange half-and-half thing, a lyric poet. 'Friday' got written while teaching an Arvon course at the Hurst in Shropshire (the playwright John Osborne's dank house, before it was exorcised by hope and made luxurious). I stood under a tree near the pond alongside which Osborne used to recline, and send his empties off to go splosh. The bottles were still there, beneath frog-spawn. I saw the image for 'A glow-in-the-dark skeleton' whilst walking near The Golden Hinde. I'm so stupid. It was only in choosing a title for a possible collection that I realised I had two glow-in-the-dark skeleton poems: prepartum and postmortem. Very often, I have no idea where what I've written has come from; almost always, though, I know exactly where it's going.

Politics / 9.11.16, p.m.

I.

When you cross a bridge over a river
you can be definite about something –
but the insides, altered, leave an after-
shock of *what*, and *what the fuck is happening*.

It would be neat if one were like the other,
and the flow and bowels met in meaning
so that out of it come mother, father,
family, house, all subordinated into song.

Instead, I am borrowing several futures
to explain yesterday's present moment
that now is cancelled, and fairly brutal
was its ending – instead, I have my fears
gradated between drowned calm, burnt torment
and the headlong lull of going foetal.

III.

Against futility, and the clasped hands
of century-separated cognoscenti –
because on dapple-pattern we all can agree,
and Beauty makes eternal amends.

The whole scaffold is entirely purposeful,
and blood-soaked, as a legitimate viewpoint.
There is an act that forces whatever it will
and cannot be *don't, you won't, you can't*.

Ease yourself into the cell, liberal,
you have prepared your own welcome
and furnished with defeats a red chamber.
This zone will always be comfortable,
and you know it to be somebody's home.
The dead are never without number.

IV.

When even a piss against a tree has
greater significance than a new move
in a familiar opening in chess –
we come to a point, sadly, where we have

to admit to ourselves that what we meant
when we insisted upon the validity
of clear and beautiful restatement
was, in fact, a truth founded on a lie.

How argument was actually quadrille,
and laws were signed on Beatrice's heart,
and even handshakes were made out of wood.
There are men who kill the men who kill
                              the men who kill,
there is a death behind the death of art,
and there is bad is caused by good.

V.

Exhaustion was the first fault, loosed
by lovers of style, the demographic
that demanded to choose where it placed
not only itself but every heretic

that had ever failed to see the funny side;
and in magazines spread self-belief
as a gospel that could be flash-fried
and served with carpaccio of beef.

Meat was a fact, this could be granted,
but butchers were not invited in, and so
butchers bowing their heads went to the lake
of all the blood they ever spilled, and counted
waves as they came in, then turned to go,
or rather turned to come back.

from 'Life Cycle'

STILLBORN

She *isn't* but she *was*.
She *wasn't* but yet *is*.

Perpetual *won't*, not *can't*.
All *didn't* and not *couldn't*.

Undone; never done.
Total knowledge, unknown.

Leaving early, arriving late.
Wholly incomplete.

One remaining plural
yet indivisible.

Entirely possible
yet infallible.

One within another;
two inside each other;
three but always either.

AMNIO

Skeleton I see and sense
Baby you become and be
Innocence lost innocence
Nothing belong to me

These things are true about you
Now they are known

TOBY LITT 141

Absolute in gesture
Say if you want a soul
Posture then imposture
I split and make you whole

These things are measured and weighed
These are your facts

And I am now what I will always ever after be.

THE GAP SO SMALL

The gap so small
        between world and child –
                no gap at all

And every fact,
        however small,
                has an impact;

your nails can cut,
        the wind can wound,
                bright light can hurt.

A tiny scrape
        upon your face –
                both of us bled.

And now it's here,
        a tiny scar:
                there will be more,
                there will be more.

There used to be a woman in this body
    not just milk

There used to be a substance to her living
    not just milk
        and carrying

There used to be a life that was outflowing
    not just milk
        and carrying
            and saying hush

There used to be a flowering of action
    not just milk
        and carrying
            and saying hush
                and putting down

There used to be a world still to discover
    not just milk
        and carrying
            and saying hush
                and putting down
                    and worrying

There used to be a world
    not just milk
        and carrying
            and saying hush
                and putting down
                    and worrying
                        and milk

Hushabye – twinkle – all – hushabye
If baby will sleep then mummy won't cry
   Mummy will tidy and mummy will clean
   Mummy will say something she didn't mean.

Hushabye – little – fall – hushabye
If baby won't sleep then mummy will cry
   Mummy will dry her tired eyes and will smile
   hoping her sweet babe will sleep in a while.

Hushabye – wonder – breaks – on my lap
If baby won't sleep then mummy will snap
   Mummy will wish that her baby were dead
   Lie down alone in the dark on the bed.

Hushabye – what you – cradle – a nap
If baby will sleep then mummy won't snap
   Mummy will weep all alone in the dark
   Take baby out for a walk in the park.

THE FIRST TURN

Now you can turn
Now you can turn yourself away from me
Now you can turn yourself

Forceful you are
Forceful you are beyond our reckoning
Forceful you are beyond

Even a god
Even a god is weak compared to you
Even a god is weak

You're everything
You're everything we fear we might destroy
You're everything we fear

The best of all
The best of all the world has ever seen
The best of all the world

I want to keep
I want to keep this time, this love, this us
I want to keep this time

I know you change
I know you change each time
Each time I look
Each time I look away

Self-Reminders

First, please don't expect them to be anything but clumsy.

Don't expect them not to break things – things, especially, which you especially don't want them to break.

Don't expect them not to be as loud as they can possibly be.

Don't expect yourself to escape breaking.

Don't expect quietness of what you probably don't call soul.

Don't expect please or thank you, even though you must constantly insist upon please and thank you.

Don't expect them to love you as you love them.

Don't expect them to understand you or even to try to understand you until you are dead.

Don't expect them, as children, to be interested in you, as you were as a child.

In fact, don't expect them to believe in your existence until you are dead.

Expect painful joys and hilarious wounds.

Expect strangers who do not know our ways here.

Expect to be wrong.

Expect their deaths, and hope to be wrong.

Awaying

When we are by ourselves, somewhere
alone – as rarely happens – we
are awkward with the double lack.
We miss the two who are elsewhere
but also the identity
we have in them. When we go back,
we think, will we have lost the knack
of being who we are? The pair,
the parents, you and me,
who hold and fix, who cope and care.
But we remain that anywhere
we go. It is us, finally.
Absence is absence, not attack
by nothingness. And we are free
to travel far, to pack, repack,
to take ourselves off anywhere.
We will be here when we come back.

Sonnet

(Like) Standing beneath a waterfall
gone dry, or sleeping through the sun's eclipse,
turning to answer no-one's call,
or pins-and-needles near your fingertips.

Uncanny, ghostly, every hopeless thing
we say – we say to try to photograph the flow
of melding, mixing, bleeding, blurring –
to really only say, *We do not know.*

Truly, a poet's words can kill,
and also truly, everybody dies;
when time holds absolutely still
you feel the tickle-touch of future eyes –

and I feel growing all within my head
the children of the resurrected dead.

Friday

There is no insight waiting
at the edge of perception
only the failure to hear birdsong
intensely enough, or look at trees
so they stay fucking looked at.

Until we are properly dead
no moment can be inhabited.
Instead, we are always glancing
sideways
at the so-called natural.

And even when we get a solo wood,
and rainfall keeping away all
but Tarkovsky's ghost,
we find only an inadequate self.

Even the botanist, the leaf-knower,
would see little beyond floating labels –
an anticipation of info-glasses,
net-retinas.

Dwell, you fucker, dwell.
Move into some faux hermitage
and stick your eyes deep in moss
for two decades. Then you might begin
to be less green.

Instead, tourist, you are ignorant,
unsated, levitating. You might as well
be the pilot of a jet, carving
                    air-valleys out of rock-valleys
from here to your usual canteen.

I imagine me for a moment made of leaves.
I imagine the forest telling itself
                    it is only a wood,
so as not to terrify me; my left
hand is being digested in the
                    stomach of a wolf;
my right hand climbs a pine until
                    it tops knowledge; most
of the rest of me has been
disembowelled by a serial killer,
the one who brought me here in the
                    guise of a fictional character.

A squirrel and another squirrel roll
my still-seeing eyeballs –
the sky, dirt, the sky, dirt.

Let us decompose – it is the just
                    thing to do,
returning Pot Noodles and Dr Pepper
                    to the earth from whence.

A glow-in-the-dark skeleton

See now, the skeleton
that I was built upon –
suspended in the dark
the waters of the dark

Each bone is blue as snow,
like icebergs from below –
suspended in the deep
the waters of the deep

They keep one moment more
the form they held before –
and now they fall apart
they start to fall apart

    My skull, like a full moon,
    all tumbling and a-swoon

    Each femur, like a whale
    or whale-boat setting sail

    Like gulls, my vertebrae
    swoop downward and away

    My finger-bones cascade –
    a shoal of sprats, afraid

    And twizzling go the ribs,
        like sail-sewn corpses, dropped from ships.

LUKE ALLAN

About halfway between Sligachan and Elgol on the Isle of Skye, there's a fork in the path. For a while another runs parallel, across the way, before veering back and reconnecting with your own. 'A Note on Walking to Elgol' recreates that walking and looking experience. 'From Marsco' does something similar: the reading is a performance for which the words and spaces are choreography. One identifies the bird from the trail of its word as it crosses the page much as the birder identifies the bird, detail by detail, as it crosses the sky.

Matsuo Bashō's haiku about a frog jumping into a pond has enjoyed many translations over the centuries. Cid Corman's 'Old pond / frog leaping / splash' is exemplary, but I have a special fondness for James Kirkup's miraculous 'pond / frog / plop!' My translation is an attempt to condense the image, or rather the language, even further. It's a bit of fun.

'Love Poem' is a vexed internal monologue, the record of a lover's vacillation between resistance and submission. It's a bit of despair. In some ways it's like the circle-poems that come later, in their search for an equivalent to the painter's blue mountains or the songwriter's fade-out, a way of saying *and so on forever*.

Pennyweight

In lifts are discussed great issues.
The indifference of pumpkins to their own faces.
Carpool etiquette. What a half mother means.
How poor chickens will poor eggs lay.
Expiration dates on water. Emily Dickinson.
Wishful thoughtlessness. The tide tables of
Lincoln. Hilda Doolittle. The crazy hours.
Umbrellas with hot handles. Underwater payments.
Chalk outline of a bomb. Carpool pumpkins.
Underwater chickens. Wishful Dickinson.
What a poor mother faces. The chalk handles!
The half hours. Crazy means. The tides of etiquette.
Hot hot Doolittle. The eggs of Lincoln.
The lifts of thought. The laid tables. The water.

A Note on Walking to Elgol

where
the path parts
follow both paths
one   one
with   with
your   your
feet   eyes
the path parts where
both paths
follow

Love Poem

you are not all that / you are
not all that you are / not all
that you are not all / that you
are not all that you / are not
all that you are not / all that
you are not all that / you are

Advice of the Assistant in a Card Shop on Enquiring Where to Find Cards without Prewritten Greetings

just on the
other side of
Thinking of you

Poetry

and, to a lesser extent,
the dogs that bathe their legs
in the lemon fields.

Lemon

This is how yellow feels between your thumbs, like a hard raindrop or a soft star. Pulsing, silent, actual. A stone with its moss on the inside, a counter-earth of spat champagne. A decorative statement about the future. If *thought is the eroticisation of consciousness* then lemons are the eroticisation of sunlight, hardwater babies growing wiser with each nap. Their pips scour the dark like owls.

A Version of Bashō

$$f$$
$$r$$
$$p \; \omega \; n \; d$$
$$g$$

Language

L=I=N=G=U=I=N=E

Variations on a Circle

to remain the grace of a curve is an invitation

falling through the water & current the against fighting &

path you can turn your back on and keep on taking the true path is the

Alexandrine

We kiss about Tom then   sleep it off. Co-fasting,
bewhited. In the pump   kin light turps-bright spoons laugh
on tiny meat hooks. Whose   head is whose we cannot
say, whose words are whose we   cannot think. Across the
curtains, the leopard-print   shadow of falling snow.

The Road Not Taken

Two roads diverged in a yellow wood
And that has made all the difference.

The Garden of Desire

flowers need flowers need flowers need flowers need

One-Word Poems for V.

A Word of Rest

forest

A Word of Care

are

A Duet

<3

A Taut Strand between Night and Morning

stay

A Word of Closure

last

Outlandia

```
        t
        s
        o
        o
        t r e
        e h o
        u s e
        i
        d
        n
        a
        l
        t
        u
        o
```

From Marsco

```
se          ae          ag          le
```

Sic Transit Gloria Mundi

On the bus home: 'Your ticket is ancient, sir.'
'And an artist's impression,' I add. As I hand it over
what he took for its face is revealed as its edge.
When he understands that its infinite surface precludes inspection,
we both laugh. 'A gentleman,' I think. 'A gentleman,' he says. 'And you,' I say.
We laugh again but harder, clutching our stomachs. I his, he mine.
We let our love be our compass.

PHOEBE POWER

'Clarsach' and 'Sleeping in his Harp-Case' belong to a sequence with the central motif of the harp. They are dream-like imaginings of strange possibilities, where the boundary between the harp and the body is unclear. In these poems, the aural texture of the poems is vital to rendering a sense of the physical, tangible body. Materiality is also key to poems which express a love of the visual. For example, 'children' is an ekphrastic poem which aims to recreate an encounter with a painting by Egon Schiele. 'Installation for a New Baby' is similarly based on an experience of looking, but in this case at an assemblage of everyday items not intended as an artwork.

In 'Es war einmal' I am interested in the possibilities of a condensed narrative. This poem retells the life-story of my Austrian grandmother, Christl, while 'Villach' records a journey in search of her hometown and relatives. Tone, syntax and prose rhythms are the material I am working with here. 'Name', 'Austrian pastorals' and 'Epiphany Night' are more fragmentary, intuitive gatherings of images. As some of the titles suggest, the latter poems in this selection are involved with the landscapes and language of Austria, in particular its rural and religious culture.

Clarsach

They lift the girl-harp in a hammock
of silver wire not to touch the ground or snap

a clavicle. Her feet are blades
not pedals. They change the key in naturals

and sharps. On the lawn, she tingles
her clitoris, and notes sprinkle with the grass-seed in the air.

Name

my grandmother's name was Chris.
ach ja – Christl.

a chrism, christ with a lemon tongue.
turquoise water inside a glass
wörthersee water
a crystal you take in your pocket or carry
touching your neck

a pair of blue and glass eyes
from a black and white portrait

a ring of yellow hair
Chris
in your army green cap

Christl
a baby lying over a stream
or the picture of a baby

sex and love with the soon-to-be accountant

REFLECTIONS: TO RELY ON IN HIS NEW JOB

sets of suits and clear
surfaces, pairs of socks in black
and black, vehicular ease, swivel
chairs, wrapped
sandwiches and selfies secure
and hairless, you may be sure of it,
card's slide out,
regular payment, her legs on screens
duplicated
you look good in black and white

WEAPONS: WITH WHICH SHE THREATENS HIM

her tongue, kissing him all over,
hands on his lovely long hands, his own
beautiful hands hurt him, her purple-coloured
self that goes and grows

with this mirrored body
I just find you attractive

get the payment, slide the card in,
black lingerie and – depend on it –
bronzer, no hair, wrapped
sandwich, swivel chair, socks,
suit, surface. She's gone.
No picture to play;
wiped memory.

children

after Egon Schiele: Stadtende

sheen and clank
snakes to this colour town
this shout! and noise –

those letterboxes squeezed
to points – faces raised
to roofs! crammed

aqua violet orange
– figures getting down
from window frames

swung open –
raised arms and bended –
scarlet and yellow trousers!

children running
verging the dark
world of tree and linelessness

calling from the roofs
and from the giant
leaves – dark green!

Epiphany Night

bells outside my wohnung
tungatungatungatung!
men in tall white hats
make a ring
hats with paper fringes
men in long white robes

then the kings
come by boat
cross the See
from dark mountains.

comes the boat
crossing dark water.

step down drei könige
in fancy robe and blackface paint

then they come with lanterns
pointing orange yellow white
pointing lantern hats then start to
multiply in all directions, starshapes,
lanterns carried everywhere
bobbing like a lake

then all the handbells stop
and ring as one
tungatungatungatungatung!
behind the See
washes at our backs

Sleeping in His Harp-Case

Harry's bed was locked up but the harp was still there, sphinx-
serena in her case. Harry slipped and shifted the robe from her
slim dark shoulders and she made no sound,
but bare strings shone white in the night
electrics. Head too large, hips narrow, feet a foetus
coiled at one end. That night, Harry slept in his heart-case.

Installation for a New Baby

HANNA LENA
29.02.2016
4285 g
51 cm

To celebrate the Hanna Lena we cut storks
from hardboard, painted white
with black outlines, orange legs and disney eyes.
We tie balloons from oberbank and peg a row
of weeny clothes, jeans and 'gros, nine
still-folded size 1 nappies, marked
each with a letter of her name.

We save soup cans, bean and veg tins
to clatter where they trail the grass,
pin a spray of rubber dummies and a
pillow, sagging rain. The doll of her
sits forward in a car seat, up-raised
polyvinyl queen. Na ja, we marker-pen,
was kann es schöneres geben
als ein kleines neues Leben?

Es war einmal

I.

A farmer was walking by a stream when he saw a basket had been left there. There was a baby, miraculously, asleep inside. Glücklich für das Kind, the soft, fine day; the slow wind didn't wake her.

II.

They called her Christl, because she came like Christ in a mean way, out of doors, and was conceived like him, mysteriously.

III.

The farmer had neighbours who, it was well-known, could not have children, and this was a great burden. The farmer's wife felt that God had laid a gift in her hands, and she was grateful for what she alone had the power to give away.

IV.

She was adopted by these neighbours. Then when she was eight, Christl's first sister was born. Heidi, with hair all over her little skull. Then came Irmgard, Günther, the twins Roswitha and Anne-Marie, and Harry.

V.

At 21 she worked in a canteen in green army uniform, serving meals to British soldiers after the war. First Frank hooked her waist and touched the bright yellow curl that emerged from her cap to rest on her cheek. One night, he stuck his dick in her. The other man came, and he wanted to take her to England and marry her, and Christl had nowhere else to bring the child, and she would not leave it by the river, so she crossed the sea.

Villach

STOP 1: ERLENDORF 54

The Erlendorf house was grey; no one came to the door.
A dark-green, electric-locked gate; thick tape on the
mouth of the newspaper tube on the mailbox. Is that a
surveillance camera? Small tubular box-eye at us, with
its slow, red-dot pulse.

We cycled asphalt Radwegs by the Autobahn and under
heavy bridges, by mineral-green streams and recy-
cling plants. Then down gravel, scuffed paths that cut
through trees and dark-green mountains, massive on
either side. A clear, turquoise lake; graffiti; warm grassy
air; spots of rain.

STOP 2: LUDWIG-WALTER STRASSE 20

Looking from the side the house was on, under the
pink faded church, a car-show called WERNER. Next to
that, a 24-hour casino and a net-cafe; on a bus-stop, a
women's underwear advert. Further along, by the cross-
ing, SCHNITZELWELT.

At the point of the address itself, a dozen new apartment
buildings in matte grey, nos 15–25 interchangeable, the
handle at 20 a big plastic mitt-shape.

Werner, my uncle told the address where my grand-
mother lived to us over the phone; he added it was
opposite a church 'with two onion domes'.

fasching

at Elli's schmankerlstube it's all
drinking and bosners.

in neukirchen it's ten a.m. and children are dancing in a pen. They're
dalmatians, indianers, cowboys with foamstick horses and goggle
eyes. Two headteachers smile and joggle in a pair, her cruella fishnet
makeup and his penguin suit, peaked beak. High loud music wrenches
in the outdoor light, rips fabric. Dance the children on.

A multicoloured snake or train of people tooting its bells and flute,
curving down the road beneath the green banks and a big sky, the
mountains.

the weather's changing

It used to be ever so hot in Austria,
not so hot now, the weather's changing, it's like in England.
When I came to England first the weather was really
warm and I thought it's warm in England nice here not so cold

because it's frosty in Austria
you get all flowers you can see out the window
you couldn't even see through because of all those ice flowers

get up in the morning freezing
get dressed straightaway make a fire
in the kitchen, we used to stay in the kitchen nice and warm there

Mary's Dreams

First Immaculata
arrived with her briefcase of tweezers, plucked
and flossed me, Felicity buffed and filed, I was
gargled, lips vaselined and sealed. They prised
my navel for disinfection but left it,
blinking, smelling of nothing.

*

On the terrace,
hair washed and dried for a sunlit breakfast,
watching the blue ocean: Anne came,
whispering *annunce, annunce*, and Teresa rinsed
my pores and slipped in the whitegold.
We sat there, after, sewing angels' wings.

*

Then Natalie with her wide white face and dark brown eyes
sat with me, rubbing my flanks
to be haylike and warm, while the animals moved in
closer and I rocked
in the weak light, under the stars like milk on ink.

Austrian pastorals

i   the lake that's black in January.

ii   an a.m. running stream,
         mineral off the Loser mountain.

iii   stepped out the car in Ratten
         to a high clear air, „Die Post", tractor.

iv   Wolfsburg, for instance, was a zone of deaf white.

v   and the Villach canal, sprayed with weed.

vi   I lived on a hill in Kärnten
         with piebald goats and barns.

vii   I'd go back to Tyrol's
         whistling river,
         I'd go to Voralberg's
         houses made from wooden feathers.

viii   I climbed forests of mountains
         and came out to insects, flowers,
         razed trees, cattle.

where I walked the smooth roads
daily, passing chickens and the ridge
above the cemetery.

THEOPHILUS KWEK

Having grown up with the even cadences of the King James Bible and Shakespeare's plays, I arrived here in 2013 to find a rhythm – of speaking and living – that was more troubling and yet more alive: an urgent, all-embracing pulse that gently remade all my expectations in favour of a younger, more diverse Britain. I quickly found community among those with different accents and persuasions, and lost an initial shyness over my Singaporean voice. In those first months, this was my country of welcome.

But other currents began to build across the country, becoming visible at the elections of 2015 and 2017, divisive leadership contests, and the EU Referendum. Visible, too, in slurs and headlines, repeated in pubs and at street corners. Some of the following poems reckon with these currents – from the rhetoric of the Brexit debate ('24.6.2016') to my own experiences of personal violence ('Occurrence'). 'Westminster' reflects on how questions of difference have become tangled with those of fear, and how to live bravely, while 'Road Cutting at Glanmire' speaks to longer-term changes which have taken place across the British Isles, and what it means to lose a landscape one knows as home.

The other poems in this set are arguments with myself, living abroad and finding belonging overseas as a son, student, and (post-)colonial subject. 'What It's Like' returns to my brief spell of National Service before leaving Singapore, with a newfound perspective on what it means to have been trained to kill for one's country at age eighteen. A trio of poems – 'Camerata', 'Requiem', and 'My Grandfather Visits Pyongyang' – revolve around my grandfather's death in 2015, while he was travelling in China. The prospect (and reality) of losing a loved one at a distance recurs in these pieces, prompting me to consider my own distance even from those who are geographically close by.

'Moving House', among the last of these poems to be written, is framed against all of these things. It takes its immediate context from my parents' decision to move out of our family home of the last decade during my time abroad, the experience of returning to a strange new room, and learning to inhabit it as my own. But such local movements might best be seen as gestures towards other, less quantifiable shifts. We inhabit new worlds, and our words must make sense of them.

Moving House

These are things that shake us in our sleep:
doors left open, drawers, the bare-backed chair
that still, without a coat, swivels gently,
books in boxes. Pictures taken down, squares
of darker paint turned over to the sun,
and above all, their wiring undone,
the lights' glass tubes put away in plastic.

Once is enough. The eye learns to plot
all of this in each new habitation,
recognise the empty room's joints, pivots,
dimensions – every house has a skeleton –
while the body learns it must carry less
from place to place, a kind of tidiness
that builds, hardens. Some call it fear,

of change, or losing what we cannot keep.
Others, experience. Truth is, it has no name
or station, and only the weight we give.
Old friend, I feel its steep tug again
this evening, across wire and lens
as you show me the house, a bare continent.
(These are things that shake us in our sleep.)

Westminster

22 March 2017

I.

Broken light, high water. Here and elsewhere
the cold thought of something beyond belief
settling into movement – an unstoppable design –
lodges in the throat, will not be sung.
We fall on words made for other means:
Visibility: four miles. More clouds than sun.

II.

Within days, it seems, this injury
will join the rim of that other, deeper cut
over which no scar can form. Unclean, unshut.
As yet it gapes distinct: flesh wound, a loss
without name and yet no easier
to reckon, its surface so bare of facts
except the act of loss itself, no choice
or distance, no motive, no face, no legend
(a mere expanse which holds the skin apart),
no way to map the way to map a way.

III.

Lines open for interchange. The earth trembles,
holds fast this steel heart, its brave circulation.
Every safe passage a jubilee. Who are they
whose paths must cross at our deepest station?

IV.

Already, without doubt, we have begun to fear
and fear the upshot of fear, the lightning and the storm.
But darkness now, which passes for calm.
                                        A prayer:

V.

For each morning that takes place unawares.
The still scalding shower. The flight of stairs.

What It's Like

How do I tell you now about the way
they placed it in his hands, a baby's weight,
just as tenderly pulled his shoulders back
to take the heave and coil, every fresh blow
leaving him sore, the sour echo of *this*
is how you kill a man?
                  It takes a man
to do that for his country, they said, and there
in the wet scrape it seemed almost true,
knowing a body's length of new earth lay
upturned, packed tight to rest his barrel on,
not daring to move, legs and torso stained
with an afternoon's digging, as ten a time
slipped away to practice advancing
from point to point, or picking up the dead,
the whole earth shattering beneath them.
Don't be scared,
                these aren't even live.
He learned to play dead, always the lightest
in the group, the one his friends would plan
to evacuate, arms crossed over one
another's to stabilise the casualty, last man
claiming his rifle where it fell *so we don't*
give the rascals anything. If you're lucky,
he's still breathing (and always, the refrain)
if not, don't move him.

It's hard to tell
the truth of it – even half, he thinks – but these
are the things he knew, or maybe knows now,
or wishes he did, is what I'm saying.

Camerata

'So great was his joy ... that Theseus did not remember to hang out the
sail which should have been a token of his safety. Aegeus, in despair at the sight,
threw himself headlong from a rock, and perished in the sea.'
– Plutarch, Life of Theseus

We left the back room of the palace locked
where the king, hearing of the fleet's approach,

had stood quickly from his untouched meal
to find his son against the sky's black sail.

Something about that room, we later felt,
foretold catastrophe. Perhaps it was what

the servant said, hours before, who found
it swept by a hand not unlike her own,

the furniture – as if by a ghost – arranged
behind fastened doors. Or what it meant

to come upon the tall, paired mirrors thrown
from their frames in fright, hiding their brazen

infinities. A cup with its cracked lip
stood on the dresser, next to where he kept

close tally for each month the boy was gone.
We could still see his numbers in the stone,

like a child's, their straight lines not touching,
Endings rubbed out where they were too long.

The last ones extended right to the floor.
And that is why we had to lock the doors.

My Grandfather Visits Pyongyang

Too late, we find among his photographs
a kingdom mostly dreamed of,

its absurd architecture where
he alighted some time in October.

Frame after frame resists comparison.
There isn't a place we've seen

that stands as still, or with the same intent
raises its glass towards heaven,

all normalcy locked within a sound
these pictures don't contain – a pitch rung

in the earth's confines, too low
for human hearing. Friends tell us to allow

ourselves the time it takes
to grieve, or whatever brings us back

to last year's long continuum,
but something stays the eye. How in some

perspectives he's already gone,
gone from the boulevards where wide-crowned

trees fill up the viewfinder,
and men and women in work clothes hover

outside our field of vision. He's
somewhere else entirely, now close,

now looking in, the disappearance
nothing more than a trick of the lens,

though we fall for it again and again.
How like him, we think,

then catch ourselves. The leaves turn
on their own impulse in our hands.

Road Cutting at Glanmire

'Gleann Maghair': the valley of ploughed land

They learned the hard way to a city's heart
was to drive a road into the mountain
like a river, lost between its own dry banks

with gravelled walls holding the earth in place
and fast-growing trees, for the wet topsoil.
A bypass. When it was finished they came

to see the cut that had been named after them,
mounting the ridge above its strange traffic
while their own valley of ploughed land rose

a stone's throw behind the black backbone
of the new highway. Far as I could tell
from the bus's window, these days the village

has a changed air, full of primary schools
and real estate. We passed a lovely church
near the auctioneer's, but without stopping

went on into Cork, taking the road which,
we were told, had been built at great cost
to shorten the journey into the city.

24.6.16

Red kites, native to Turkey, Morocco, and parts of Europe,
were declared 'vermin' by the English crown and hunted nearly to extinction.
They were successfully reintroduced to the UK in 1989.

No red kites over the field this morning.
However hard I looked, I could not find

a single cresting pair, their high crosses
invisible – as if unpitched from the grass.

No dry swoop, no sounding. No clatter from
morning's fed sparrows rising in alarm,

no hare's carcass eaten behind our wall,
nothing astir. No courting on the fell

in curious patterns, no stumbling display
of swift shadows bending above the Wye.

No haunt. No song. Only the heaven's blue
graceless fire, and then as a ghost pursued

across a moor, the hunting-horn's burly
cry
                    crucify, crucify, crucify.

Requiem

Gong-gong, 1936–2015

You met us again in the outer room.
White bone in miniature, glazed earth
parting the skull's cracked continents.

With love's red cloth covering the bowl,
we lined up one by one to send you home.
A pair of hands took each broken part

and joined it with the others in the pile
so the pieces belonged as they were laid,
tibia, sternum, pelvis, patella

nook to nook, against the plain design.
In cupped fingers we scooped the fire-
tempered sand, a cloud of chalk

over the precious hill. You said nothing,
content that we should have our ways of loss,
our sifted, falling silences, the plunge

of numbed hands under frigid water.
Teach me now to love, at their frayed edges
the left-behind, their washed and ashen fingers.

Occurrence

Thames Valley Police, no. 43 150 33 1197

'6.35 p.m. on 23rd November, 2015: the victim was struck on the face with a
metal rod by men in an unidentified car, on Oriel Square, breaking his glasses.
No assailant could be traced.'

Nothing much then, now nearly unseen –
a cut beneath the eye. A bruise, fading
to skin, frown and furrow, fine print. How

soon the body grieves, forgives how easily
it gives. Already these marks are marks
of other things. Sleepless lines that mar

an early frost. Fields turned for planting,
sandstone shorn against the river's brink.
A fishhook's incline, the doubling pitch

of flight like a whaler's reckoning. In
the hollow of a bridge the water leaves
no scar, only trembling. A sound gone

as if from a whipped bowstring, between
where the arrow flies and, at each end,
thread spliced so as to pucker wood: the eyes.

Dead Man's Savings Won't Go to Wife

'Ms Diao, a Chinese national ... claimed to love Mr Soon and to meet him for dinner about once a week, but could not say why she loved him, and claimed they would eat fish, when Mr Soon did not.' – The Straits Times, 8 September 2016

How could I explain? Your first glance
Was that of an old lover. All guilt,
No charm. As I washed the breakfast things
You struggled with your shirt, belt,

Looked away when I knelt
To lace your shoes. Those mornings
Turned out to be my favourite –
Us two in the park downstairs,

Your arm on mine as joggers passed,
Wings touching as we flew. Months
Wore on. You ate little, spoke less,
But still I knew you'd *give a thousand coins*

For *my smile,* the way you'd sit
By the door waiting, or press a little extra
Into my palm as I went to market
For threadfin or garoupa,

Something for myself. For you this
Was enough, an extravagance, nearly,
Of joy. And I? *I loved the house*
And the crows that nested there,

The missed appointments, separate beds,
How you always left the radio on.
In the end, they said,
You gave no last instructions,

So it wasn't clear my claim was genuine.
That, I tried not to mind.
I wish you'd told them how much this would mean.
One who knows my voice is hard to find.

* Italics denote loose translations of Chinese idioms for love:
一见如故, 比翼双飞, 千金买笑, 爱屋及乌, 知音难觅

Blue

Years later, I saw in the Ashmolean
precious plates, fine porcelain

of the best handiwork, that stood
down the aisle on the first floor

in their blue cases. Some of them by then
I already knew by heart, having gone

to school in the refurbished building
where we painted, one year, a semblance

of a low Victorian house that sat out of reach
as our bus-route narrowed to a bridge.

Others I had never seen, but were the twins
of a bright, winding city where I spent

hours salvaged from school and home
with my own widening strides marking time,

close likenesses copied onto each gleaming
dish from Calcutta and Penang.

Behind Grandmother's house there was once
a factory where, in her motley tongue,

she told me they used to blow blue glass
for windowpanes, wine bottles, flasks.

I pressed my hands to the cabinet
full of china, and dreamt that I could touch

the tea services, with their beautiful necks
too thin, too tall for proper use.

KATHERINE HORREX

Yehuda Amichai made the claim that 'all poetry is political ... even if a poet sits in a glass house drinking tea, it reflects politics.' Regarding politics, I once read a selection of my work, including my poem 'Brexit', and one of the poets that followed made a comment on stage about 'how easy it is to write political poems'. My awareness of how political that comment was allows me to take it with a pinch of salt; the Brexit vote and its outcome was always going to be very interesting to me as someone who was at the time the only British person living in a building of fifty residents, in Manchester. I was a foreigner in my own home and having a great time, so the concerns of Brexiteers in my former hometown of Hull – such as 'that twenty Polish families had recently moved into the area' – were disgusting to me, if not particularly surprising, and formed the basis of my portrait of Brexit as a place.

Other things I wrote at this time explore the idea that a poet's connection to 'the muse' can be plural; that it might be harmful if inspiration were attached to one thing only. In 'Four Muses' – written in tercets, not just to provoke the fury of readers who would want it written in quatrains, but because tercets can be very good at buoying rapid streams of images – I wanted to acknowledge a set of grim, but interesting, environmental truths. Microclimates. Unhelpful forms of education. The need to address unusual and unlikeable things in society grew alongside my interest in Jon Ronson's gonzo journalism; his exploration of extremists in *Them* and the deranged, damaged army operatives he interviewed for *The Men who Stare at Goats*.

As regards 'Goat Fell', an interesting name and beautiful scenery might be inspiration enough for writing a poem but it was not until the death of a friend I made during a trip to the Isle of Arran that I felt a need to do so – perhaps because the hill's apparent timelessness, when set against the transitory nature of human existence, provided enough conflict to make it especially worth exploring in language.

Goat Fell's history as the scene of a murder in the late 1800s (the murder of Edwin Rose) meant that it seemed all the more apt as a framework for elegy. The idea that the hill might be haunted in some way meant that the otherworldliness of its name and setting could be explored via psychological and spiritual phenomena, rather than the plainly pastoral. My aim with the piece was to put language in the foreground, to create shifts in register and movements towards dialect that might resonate with shifts in geography, altitude and mental state, in relation to the overcoming of an obstacle, physical or otherwise.

Brexit

The city has been stamped with leaves
and is a mail bag, waiting to be posted somewhere.
Houses, on a hillside, stacked like letters
spilling over so the wind can almost snatch them.

Its streets are grit filled markings on a shoe sole
cambering uneasily at the heel
and worn into themselves like grafted skin.
The tarmac has a greasy sheen.

Only people's backs, hunched towards shopping,
confirm life happens here, wrapped in cagoules,
people personable as tents zipped shut,
canvas for the rain to write on.

They lean into windows lit like oilseed,
believe they're holding something by its horns.
Their houses ache like letters that leave something bad unsaid.
But now the whole world knows their thoughts.

Theirs was only the stale and temporary discretion
of booths at a polling station.
Houses on the hillside turn to banners
filling with the wind, which will not take them far.

Afraid is a Town

Where mills made largely of lead
snuff out your phone signal as fast
as an all-seeing foreman,

where midnight footfall
three houses down
sounds like intruders in your home,

where what I thought was the shadowy clatter of hooves,
threatening to lend more furlongs to the dark,
was a paint tin rolling in the street,

where the scene of Lowry's *The Chapel*
looks even more 'down at heel'
now weed-clogged, cracked and chapel-less,

where, on a hill, a church bell
hungers, behind wooden slats, for every hour
to shake off festering bats,

where, although no one's there, you feel
fists, or knives, waiting to meet you in anger,
throbbing in pockets of air,

where people still say the rain
carries radioactive traces,
landing on your head even as you watch

a hundred paper lanterns descend
delicately round a kink in the cloud
over a monument that honours the dead.

Polycystic

Ultrasound shows them:
moth holes
in the vacuum of the ovum.

Medics refer to 'strings of pearls',
some of which teethe,
their tissue is that much an assortment of cells,

casting out hair and bone to become
small sacks of offerings stored
in the tract.

Even without the scan wand
painting this wall before children,
the cysts are clear now,
grounding me like pebbles.

But I can leave the hospital for home
where I don't keep
plants in urns, their roots all stoppered
with gravel.

I'll try to induce myself,
conducting the passage of a lunar month
through measures of darkness and light.

I'm waiting for my body to snow.

Grey Natural Light

It breaks through voile curtains
and stains like tannin leaching into a cup;

(The voile bunches like tissue paper
strewn by an elephant.)

Carbon filters into rooms
invisibly, on the back of the world's breath.

Dioxide. It is not unexpected.
Nor is it hindered; almost every car

trails ashes down the roads' long
crawl of *grau, grau, grau*. Not much

today it seems will grow but we may dig
for graphite, paint elephants in the sky azure.

Four Muses

What to say to my muse the power plant
who makes auras for the city's night hours
with a sputter of wattage and volts?

What to say to my muse the steelworks,
who sends hot blasts down the standpipe
for fig trees to thrive in?

What to say of the pigments
rolled out in testing chambers
by my latest muse the chemical plant?

What to say when the power plant
hums and clicks and shines
like a fairylit woodwind instrument?

What to say when the belting out
of playground pieces gives way
to the making of girders for steelworks?

What to say when McBrides carpets the Roch
and makes soft, six-foot dams
out of flammable detergent?

How to contain them all
and do justice to their invention of
and disregard for protocol,

how to juggle their sweltering egos
when I walk where figs
leave oily splats on the towpath,

street lamps turn pale in daylight
and latex dries in a bucket slung round
a rubber plant's tapped green trunk?

Goat Fell

Only after living in its shadow for a month
can I say that its attraction has worn off,
that I went there once or twice
seeking a river locals mentioned
not long after I arrived,

nose raw with the churchy strangeness
of water underfoot and the valley
closing over like a hand. My boots
were sucked by moss and a slip in the mud
nearly had me kneeling

as if I were a pilgrim at the island's altar.
More like it was the butcher's block
in the craggiest backstory of this particular ayr
and what I'd heard before meant that halfway up,
when the wind ran round a slate grey howff,

it seemed to whisper 'Rose, Rose.' The way a boiler
in an old, old house takes on the voice
of someone who's not there. Now I do not want to go
into that cold mountain dream with feet scrying
for the summit in the screes and murder in the fellside's bones.

Lapwings in Fallowfield

They sit with the road's oily
tang in their nares,
their bodies like helmets in grass.

Younger ones look like soil
upon snow and nest
in the adults' thick feathers.

My sister and I at somebody's
wedding, when we hid
under somebody's dress.

Moon Jar and Moon dark

I wouldn't think to hide something in such a lampish vessel
as the moon jar, its two hemispheres of bright clay joined
for the storage of rice, soy sauce and alcohol.
Porcelain is not especially given to the clandestine,
though here it calls something to my mind
of the old Chesire noun for a wife's nest egg,
                            hidden from her husband.

Buttermere

When the lake came for us
a dark hue zipped across it
like a tent's outer shell being shut.
It stung us as it rose
from out of the stillness
drawing the surface over us.

I swam in it that afternoon
which was warm and perfectly current-less
but for the wind, rushing to knock me,
bidding that I pray

to the pebbles,
the shale and broken bottles,
a trip-me-up dirty old rope
mooring the shadows
for god knows how long.

Feet off the grit floor it was fine.
The lake stirred in fits
but was no real threat to movement further out,

the body a bow that way,
rolling through the water's cool slaps,
delving for the other side.

But, out there alone,
and not a quarter of the way across,
I found I had to turn

for fear I'd meet the pucker
of miles-dark depths
and things touched fearlessly
by water only.

I wanted no part in that journey.

Waking in Twos

A clock knocks time
between four walls
where we lie caught up
in the excellent rejection
of all company but each other's,
immune to the pendulum
as if it were the call
of animals elsewhere –
cockerels crowing about
unfinished revolution,
so that whoever still sleeps, or slept,
is on infinite alert, half consciously. Not us.
Next door's farm winds down,
its owner dead by his own gun
for some days now. Not us
and lorries light our room
with the colours of commerce.

Wood Frog

There is nonchalance in the veins
of the roses you gave me.
Their heads hang stiffly
over dried-out stalks.
I forgot to water them, or rather
thought I'd watered them but hadn't.

Now that I have means nothing,
though the stems puff and the heads
begin to lift, trembling as ice
trembles in the early yards of spring.
Though the buds begin to chafe
with light and grow

the way a wood frog sparks
itself to life after a full winter
cased in tundra, its solid black
nut of a body soft again,
eyes lifting from the thaw
of its torso in answer to the storm

in its cells. No such urgency
is found in a vase, though there may
have been a hope in giving,
in the short brightening of this room
where a corolla frowningly describes
a person's heart.

JAMES LEO MCASKILL

These selected poems have some features in common. Perhaps immediately obvious is their occasional use of the two-line stanza. This form gives the poems a uniformity of appearance yet it is put to different use in each. 'Days' utilises the couplet's ability to create comparison. Two seemingly disparate images side by side in a repeating process. Since these images and events, which cover the historical, social and personal, are all given in the present tense, the effect is to condense time, to remove from it a linear progression. 'Coming Thunder', a loose sonnet, plays on this form's inherent capacity to create and emphasise the notion of coupling. Its effect is visual as well as symbolic. In 'The Norseman's First Summer', a poem which mixes plain English and fragmentary Old Norse, the form is used to control the poem's pace, something crucial when two languages are in balance. And lastly in Labour, a poem exhaustively taxonomical, the form shapes the poem into a kind of ladder, each stanza break aiding the reader's descent as well as their re-ascent after the poem's final couplet.

In other works, such as 'Coffee Morning' and 'from Lasts', form is less fixed. 'Coffee Morning' tumbles from its initial conversational beginning, getting curt and sudden by the close. 'from Lasts', being an extract from a longer work, has a narrative drive, so follows the nature of that narrative. In 'Odessa', the first section of the poem, the narrative voice uses stanzas and stanza changes to progress, invert or encase individual thoughts and moments. Whereas later in the poem, in 'Vicissitude', each stanza exists to present complete or incomplete acts, a kind of poetical to-do list.

Thematically these nine poems are a somewhat broad nonagon held together by common concerns such as time, image and speech. There is a certain consideration for history as well as for the contemporary; with how things are said as well as how things are seen. Yet, perhaps most significantly, they are as different as they are similar, and are meant to be read as such.

Days

They are cleaning the bells in Viterbe.
The bus is near Urbino.

The oak-green cascades are falling in the North-West.
A sheep is watching the sea hit the rocks.

Rick is doing his loft in the sunset.
Brown clouds are above Nantong.

Justinian bathes, and drinks the water he bathes in.
A film projector loops *Gone with the Wind*.

Coventry is twinned with Dresden.
Sarcasm is invented, then contravened.

The fish eat at a shipwreck of fingers and gold.
A century turns to another.

Laura never looks the same in any two pictures.
Hiro and his wife are at a weighing.

The unpeopled earth is illuminated by a billion stars.
The toes are going through the grapes.

Nobody ever bothers to call.
The people in the rainforest have never heard of the Portuguese.

Usman is feeling tired but doesn't know why.
They make the area into a national park.

A child's clitoris is removed with a piece of glass.
Gin is invented.

In the basement there are things no one should see.
Something is shimmering on the water, in the air.

Charlemagne regrets his trip to Rome.
Natale can only see his kids at weekends.

Women and Men rebuild the cathedral at Chartres.
They go out on the water in the rain.

What his father tells him, he tells his son.
The plane crashes in Munich in the snow.

Her waist bends to the will of her clothing.
The wanderers arrive at Skelig Michael.

They wait and wait but he never comes.
People scatter determinedly around the continents.

Ira wakes from a confusing dream.
The ancestors line the longhouse and sing

sing
sing.

Coming Thunder

When we stole the eggs from the barn that June
you said we held life in our hands.

Untrue I said as I carried a near score
in my upturned t-shirt.

And even if I could hold one
it would never get born

not in those hands that you let
be put on you

or in the grass nest we made
smelling of piss-yellow sunshine

or by us two, old enough to ourselves
be parents

but still going around like foxes
wasting things other people might like to use.

Joke

for C.C.

I said I was
nella Campagna, nella campagna
that was my joke

as you took the car off the road
and wordlessly through green branches
to where wide earth

was silent by vines and horse houses.
You put me inside you
under your skirts
and that's when I thought of my joke.

Sometimes the simplest way is silence
the car so hot I could only make out
horse sounds in the back
our two bodies moving beyond a joke.

Coffee Morning

What a perfect morning you say
the milk's gone bad.

I smell it because I want to know
how bad

Very you say and we are
wrinkled noses and frowns
and black coffee drinkers now

I choose a path that goes far down
that does not reek
nor connect to home

to bury
what will grow white
soft and wet

yet I reach a stump
full with ants and dry
and spill its top with our milk.

The ants sail and roll.
This is their problem now.

Baghdad

What words come from jealousy?
The walls of encircling palaces
and a barely traceable line.

The market became many markets
as the Prophet became many men,
and, at the hand of the cloth seller,
the Caliph whispered
I am not he.

The disguise of a distempered Araby.
The world from Cairo to Bukhara.

At the highest point,
the stone heart of the city,
the richness of a religious heart
turned.

The Norseman's First Summer

Fok-pykkr, in rás sæti
the leave-gone from water mountain

day, day, day, black-day, ne slæpe,
see dust yellow, push, push, live,

vision, ne boll, kið, geit, geit-punnr, live
tree small, mansize, unstrong

green maker yellow oil and hot, beard
and wine hot. Kið, geit, tree-small

unsnowed, unvile land, fok-punnr
wifmen-light, light wimmen, housers

uncolded, unfat, black, dark-soft
yellow-oil wifmen in this tree-small.

Fok leg-spread by skeið, vǫlvur
in song-lag, ear-turners dream

in day-passion, skeið to edgewater
to vǫlvur, fok-pykkr and slæpe.

Radix (Augury)

The future is tomatoes
you know will grow fat

red and different
on the budding vine

you lace yourself –
a spider lacing a trap –

to catch the future
tense. All else is now

perpetually, the tomatos,
too, are now

as you throw

what was once
going to happen.

Labour

They say it is the oldest profession.
Older than the sea-vacuuming fishermen;

the proverbial sheep-and-goatherds;
the sweat-faced smiths and smith's apprentice

unable to find a girlfriend on an unsalaried
internship, sharing a room south of the river;

the milliners; the winemakers; the builders,
dragging slop mud into squares of dry mudbrick

for a mosque and a house and a brothel;
the accountants; the taxmen; all those

of jobs immoral enough to bring about
religious conversion, a change of heart,

hold a burgeoning civilisation together;
the cross-makers; the athletes;

those who did things with wood
before the Romans; the transubstantiationists;

the producers of religions and religious stories;
the road-footed messengers;

the breakers of horses and donkeys;
the finders of navigable routes over mountains

through seas and forests and marshland;
the stalkers, approachers and fellers of deer

elephant, buffalo, whale and whale shark;
the singers; the incorrigible upright walkers.

Well, with all this work being done
why shouldn't a woman have a job?

from Lasts

I. ODESSA

I have memories of the day I knew my future
that I would marry a soldier
in the wax-fizzing shapes
you cannot read yourself –
premonitions are for someone else
to see – and I balled all night
at the certainty of my sleeping
curled around a rifle
a horse and sword at the breakfast table
his steady hand decapitating my egg
with the functional twitch
of putting down bodies not yet dead

yet it's a growth industry
and sure to keep me good and safe
and clothed in the modernest ways
women and men at the tea trays
day and night performances
all the staples house and life require

unsnowed hours in the pleasure grounds
mind-projected flowers in the rush
a finger to my mouth to hush
my breathing words of all the planted names
and patterns of pine shadows

that never go out of leaf. And when my daughter sleeps
to her ear I will sing
the sound the water makes in Odessa
each note a star in the star-ecstatic sky.

I am sure I know how I will die –
when all the people of the world come to Odessa
filing secretly, secretly to themselves,
down the Potemkin steps, idempotent
and glad toward the sea, to wash there,
to feel how good cold can be
when you have no cares for drowning
nor deep water's charming
murmur of mouth-bubbling water.
I will tell these moments to my daughter

when drip drop they all go over
the great populations in coats and hats
deliberate dress for deliberate acts
bringing the water back.

He was thin and cautious as a cat
surly behind a baroque moustache
spine like a brushstroke
and when he spoke
all good and hiding complexity
I waited

for the day he walked me round by the arm
the ocean horse-kicking itself calm
and black
as such days.

He was quick to talk of love
and not shy to reach
his body up and over me,

waves reaching out above the sea
and sand-plumes of wind
below my hands.

He fascinated in the salon
walls clad with conversation
a nice line of argument when asked
of bears he killed
in the north
in the past
leaning in the inside fire shine.

The pleasure it seems was only mine
half a season of love shaped with time
and victory beauty refinement dense
as a bad cold.

I will tell my daughter this when I am old.

II. LAKE CHAD

Bedoved above the silent water
there are nonagons of vulture
sense-hovering, escaping the wetlands
and current social limitations, for Niger,
for the Air mountains, for bones to pick.

V. VICISSITUDE

In chintz along the San Martine she promised
she would be back

when all the death-houses were hotels
and each new language
from the inflowing people
was prismed into a single tongue

when the one-eyed boys joined hands
and shared the job of seeing
heavy changes,
the repeating apocalypse of Tuesdays

when all we had to do
had been done.

The waist-high water split her like a question
to an answer I had already begun.

VI. SOUTHERN HEMISPHERE
I showed her the emptiest half of the world
islands snow-curled in white sand
whales filling whale throats
time-old fishing and freight boats
lungs of wind below the world ceiling

we made good our living
two stones anchoring beach towels
head-flipped centimes for dolmades
taro and manioc soft
salt lips drunk of kava
laplap in the nakamal doorway.
We spoke much of the night and looked across the islands

to Menelaus in his war-fond tupenu
tattooed with all accompaniments of rank
the top half of his body big and out
lumping his man-breasted power all about
ready to launch a thousand-canoed assault
as though to peg a hurricane to the ground.
Each and every night behind the sound
of men in low-lying warboats just because
he couldn't fight a war for only love.

I showed her the emptiest half of the world
festooned in rare birds and space
half her face
upon the pillowcase
the backward moving ceiling fan
reflecting helicopters on the divan
to all the tired nights –

to all the tired nights I prayed
as in São Cristóvão, as in that golden glade
of tired nights
of carrying her upon my back, sleeping
in the angled mountain rain
in a house of mud-daubed walls and skin
and llama in the drunken mist
of names of rain and words for raining
and ancestors vanished for never having lived.

The ever-forest canopy dropped our eyelids
till all the hours and all the days reversed
and all the warboats journeyed back in time
and Qusqu raised its blood hearts to the fire
and green in golden magic gods returned
and tapestries of spiders reeled and burned
to celebrate the world-destroying world.

We know now what we never learned, how
expressible in her throat were lyric words
she heard each night from song-wing birds
who fly and fly sunlight around the world
till inexpressible in her throat we heard
the brown voiced Ucayali
the infinity of trees where no one ever dies.

ROWLAND BAGNALL

Many of the these poems are constructed from the bits and pieces of experience – loose words and phrases, persistent images and thoughts – that decided to stick around, for whatever reason, after the party. Eventually, a group of them will draw together and become a scaffold, which can then be used to make a poem. I'm interested in glitches, particularly when language, sense, and memory go wrong, and in the different ways of using/abusing these malfunctions. I also think a lot about the images we keep, and how we can't really control the way those images relate, or what can happen to them once they're set loose in the Jungle Gym of our imaginations. It's possible that my writing has something in common with collage's particular species of vandalism, although this hasn't been a conscious choice. I do find lots to write about in visual art and film, however, which I suppose will be apparent here. More often than not, the shape of a poem tends to determine itself, so I usually end up paying closer attention to its sounds, its rhythms, and its repetitions. Occasionally, during the process of writing, a poem will begin to feed upon itself, biting off its fingernails, which I expect relates to glitches, too; something like this is happening in 'Hothouse'. I like to think of these poems as having nothing to do with me personally, but get the feeling this is not the case.

Subtitle

The poem keeps away when I can't see or there's nothing to see

We were looking at what seemed to be nothing,
which was, in fact, nothing, gradually and suddenly gone,
fascinating the way footage of a car-crash is fascinating,
or the wrongful demolition of a hospital, beautiful.
There must be a better word for just exactly the wrong
word for 'accident', or 'the almost complete absence
of light from a room lighted only by the static from
a television set', waiting to be found and used –
more or less visible – in the retranslation of a film
in which the English from the mouths of the protagonist's
enemy's goons can be seen, as if intruding on itself,
surfacing too quickly to the surface of the screen
with the almost complete absence of its retranslation,
an always-certain interruption of an interruption.

What if that sky's a ceiling? That ceiling, a window
not quite closed or opening? What if *What if that sky's
a ceiling?*'s a ceiling, but might as well've been clouds
emerging from, or falling behind, a sky full of clouds?
I was surprised to feel guilty, if guilty; ashamed of my
shame, if shamed. On the air I recognised a word
in Czech, left untranslated at the bottom of the screen,
appearing in italics as it was, its meaning lost, assumed
or untranslatable in kind, kind of non-existent, like a sky,
painted or projected on an off-white ceiling. After
the dust cleared, the buildings resurfacing as a wave,
dormant for miles, resurfaces towards a peopled beach,
the room, more or less visible, seemed to slowly sink,
us still looking at nothing, and then nothing again.

Sonnet

Eating at a restaurant where the food was all described as *young* and *tender*,
you said that you had 'absolutely nothing' to say, chewing chewing-gum.

Without looking at each other, I said, 'Did I ever tell you,' (knowing
I hadn't), and proceeded to tell the same old story, except that I couldn't
   remember

it properly, thinking for a second that it might have turned out differently,
which it didn't, which isn't to say I'd change a thing, trying to decide
   what colour

I'd call the ceiling if forced to call it a colour. On/After the day it happened,
something moved in the darkness and I stamped on it, all morning.

What would it feel like to undergo electrocution? What was/Was that
a hovercraft? Dissecting seafood, you explained how if you walk behind

someone on a deserted street you only have to quicken your step slightly
to instil fear in the person that you're following, or about the developing

technological capabilities of rendering the artificial 'real'. 'When you empty
water into a vessel and then shatter the vessel the water stays, just for a
   moment,

where it was, no longer slightly different from itself.' Was that blood
in the mayonnaise? I thought. Was that window blue on purpose?

Like a thought cut into speech, or black line next to nothing, everything
   echoes
and then the echoes meld, like unwittingly walking into a place you've
   just left

and not realising it's the same place, or knowing why you've chosen to go in.
Can't you see a face? Can't you catch a brief glimpse from a passing train,

like the trains you can't see in a Hopper painting? On/Before the day it
    happened,
we watched that episode of *The Sopranos* (1999–2007) where Tony dreams

he's running from an angry mob and ends up riding on his horse inside
    the house
he used to live in with Carmela. You laughed the way you laugh when you're

not really paying attention, so I imagined you getting shot in an
    assassination
meant for someone else and went upstairs to hold on to the bathroom
    railings.

Without looking at each other, something moved in the darkness. Without
    saying
anything, I thought for a second that it could have turned out differently.

Kopfkino

I felt lonely, like I'd missed the boat, / or I'd found the boat and it was deserted

Like the moment between knowing you might nearly jump
and actually nearly jumping, I considered half-undressing
an imagined Joan of Arc, approaching to the stake with faceless
soldiers and a crowd of muted children like the children in the foreground
of a Lowry painting. The only thing she could get through to me was,
It's not that I'm afraid to die, I just don't want to be there when it happens,
which, in the circumstances, we all agreed was pretty funny.

It was one of those rare experiences where you move into rain that's already
falling somewhere else. In another place, but a place exactly the same
as this, I thought about the bit in *Fargo* (1996) where Steve Buscemi gets
stuffed into the wood-chipper until only his feet are left, imagining what
    that

must be like those first few seconds you're alive, and whether you'd bleed
    out
on the snow or just lose consciousness immediately, the way some people
suddenly lose consciousness when a rollercoaster hits a loop-the-loop.

Standing before Manet's *Execution of Maximillian* (c.1867) in the National
Gallery – damaged into sections pieced together on a canvas in the 1990s –
I watched the shooting in full view, despite the missing fragments on the
    wall.
The Emperor clasped the hand of his companion as an officer, hardly visible,
signalled to the firing squad, vanishing behind a stage-effect of rifle smoke.
I decided that it was the best painting I had seen for a long time,
despite having seen it before somewhere, and missed it.

Someone laughed the kind of unexpected laughter that occurs
when you realise how ridiculous it is that you're disposing of a body
rolled inside a Turkish carpet, or hacked-to-bits and wrapped inside
a plastic bag to keep the blood from spoiling the upholstery in your car.
I could see a kayak heading for a hurricane, which was annoying
because I was in the kayak and I couldn't swim, or think of how
to get myself to shore. *Life is full of misery, loneliness, and suffering –*

and it's all over much too soon, I said aloud, which was annoying
because, in the circumstances, it would've been a lot funnier
if there'd been someone there to hear me say it. I could imagine
swirling around, not sure what it was that would actually kill me
but certain there'd be no way out of this one. As everything refocused,
like only realising that someone has left a room when they re-enter it,
it was late afternoon and the sun was in my eyes so I hadn't seen anything.

Viewpoint

In *Rear Window* (1954), Alfred Hitchcock suddenly looks at us
through the glass frame of an apartment penthouse, somehow
somewhere other than behind the camera's lens – viewed from
the perspective of James Stewart's binoculars – all but invisible
to anyone who doesn't know it's him. *Always make the audience
suffer as much as possible*, I thought, rains beginning on the roof.

From up here I could see a skydiver looking backwards at a plane
as if it was falling away from him and not the other way around.
The air was the same temperature as I was, still breathable and
warm but lightly thickening with something else, like vapours
pouring slowly from a car's exhaust. Away to the right I swore
I could see the monstrously reclining figures of a sculpture park,

misshapen and decayed, the stones displaying marks left by
the hurricanes of several years ago. Around the moment of
deployment, the parachutist feels a brief instance of shock
between the pulling of the ripcord and successful opening
of the main canopy. Convinced the mechanism has finally
failed, he tries to recall a succession of emergency techniques

before – at last – the canvas swells, jerking freefall to violent
and relieving halt. Throughout the film, a pianist composes
a song called 'Lisa'. His voice is never heard, appearing only
in long shots through the window. He seems to live alone but
for the brief appearence of the filmmaker standing several
feet behind him, winding an old clock on the mantelpiece.

In the Funhouse

In *Superman: the Movie* (1978), Superman turns back time
by flying backwards round the globe. We see a rockslide
happen in reverse as Lois Lane emerges from the sinkhole
she's been crushed to death in, meaning that she never died
at all. In the Funhouse, a mirror shows me stretched, my head
caved in, the sole survivor of some hilarious near-fatal collision.

Halfway down an artificial indoor beach (running along a back
wall painted with what looked suspiciously like the Normandy
landings: upturned bodies on the sand, bits of bodies in the sea,
the constant sound of waves and cartoon screaming and explosions
coming from a speaker hidden somewhere in the ceiling) I wondered
if my limbs had returned to normal. The floor began to move in

circles at different speeds. The walls pressed slowly in around me.
Next door, a neon light shone on a plastic Christopher Reeve.
I made my hand into a fist and thrust it out in front of me which
did nothing, which didn't surprise anyone in the room, which
was only me, which didn't surprise anyone in the room. Crawling
through a tunnel on my hands and knees, I imagined Superman

saving me in a succession of perilous displays: trapped in the back
of a mechanically compressing car on a junkyard conveyor belt;
falling head-first from the topmost floor of a collapsing holiday
resort in Spain; cocooned in ropes and laid out on a railway track
by thugs. As I emerged, I was suddenly reminded of a scene in
a film, though couldn't remember which scene, or which film.

Evening in Colorado

Something unwinds and breaks, spilling glass across the room.
It takes time to establish that a thing's not there – noise, stars,
excitement, grief – like the shutting-off of certain lights.

I remembered having been to Florida as a child,
but could only really summon up the glare of heat on roads,
a beach, and a skyline of durationless hotels.

We had a rental car with cruise control, which I remember
thinking drove itself. But now from up here I see everything,
the city like a signal on the verge of fading out.

I drank a bottle of 'tropical' flavoured liquid and sat down
on the bed, thinking about my brothers – thousands
of miles away in several directions – staring through

the window at a bright display of grand pianos,
an old cinema, and the empty space a building used to be.
A group of children ran around through jets of water.

Something unwinds and breaks: like a morning? silence?
cables? arms? During the night I woke up to an accident
and lay there motionless beneath the ceiling fan.

I–5 North

who is more naked / than the man / yelling, 'Hey, I'm home!' / to an empty house?

About an hour from Los Angeles we pass the spot
where two weeks previously I'd seen the aftermath
of a collision. Two firefighters were joking
around, spraying suppressive foam across
dark patches of earth that had until recently been
on fire; the whole thing seemed meticulously staged.

In a photograph a man is washing blood away from
fish. A heavy knife is in the sink. His hands are
sticking to the insides of his latex gloves.
The sun grinds landscapes to a halt. It strips them
bare and crumples them like fabric, which sounds
like something Robert Hass would write.

Another picture shows a broken statue.
Large sections of the stone are missing so the stone
beneath becomes the statue's surface. The figure
looks deformed, like she's been caught in an explosion.
Out to my left, the orange groves give way to
massive oil fields; the lakes resolve a contradiction.

Driving back down to the city from
Sequoia National Park, I saw we must've passed
by the collision site again. I'd hoped that this
would turn itself into something that felt more
profound, like stepping into water
the same temperature as air.

Jet Ski

Emerging switch-eyed from the undergrowth
into an evening that has just arrived but where there's still
and mainly light, at least for now, withdrawing like receding rooms,
the trees losing distinction like the faces in a crowd that's running
to or from an incident you haven't yet heard news about,
or single voices drowned out in a vast simultaneity of voices,
we see a guy pass on a jet ski, and I wonder what
he's thinking, if he's happy, where he's going, or whether
he's forgiven himself, truly, for the thing he's most ashamed.
Each thought feels like the answer to a question that
I've not been asked: the images of solar flares; religious
martyrs' final words; the knowledge that you're not where
you're supposed to be; another world, a bit like this.

As if to say, *Well, what did you expect?*, shrugging off
each revelation like a soothsayer who knows he's right,
the jet ski rider disappeared into the mists across the bay
from us. I felt an urge to drop my things and go, to follow
him and start a new life in the sun, hearing his voice say,
That's what I did, Baby, and look what happened to me, the wake
waves of his jet ski gently lapping on the pebbled shore.

A Few Interiors

This time we're seeing from a hiding place,
pointing stuff out – the window, heater,
Boston fern – in the interior, which is a picture
in the corner of the room, a bit unfinished,
as if an upset woman might burst in holding a letter
any minute now. The walls are white,
like a museum. There's ivy growing out from
not the top shelf but the next one down
and water in a half-drunk plastic bottle on the desk.
Within the water there's another image of the room,
reflected, bending at the sides. You can't quite see it
yet because we're standing too far
from the door, not entering for fear of
causing a disturbance. In the reflection
there's a third person as well,
but when I turn around they've gone
which is a joke I've played on you before.

The house is built among some pine trees
that are being cut down to make timber frames.
You sometimes hear a rifle going off
some miles away, which is a deer shot through
the neck, or just some people
killing time by firing hot rounds at the air.
Tonight there's an eclipse, but it's too cloudy
out for us to know. Instead, the empty
stairwells and the armchairs start to creak.

Divining through the long grass on the island
we find bone. Perhaps, you say, the bone's a sign,
a way of answering a problem that you're spending
your days struggling through. Back in the kitchen
it looks strange among the cutlery and tiles

and I resent not knowing which part
of which animal it shaped so throw it out
after a day or two.

A man arrives holding a lute.
The young girl sitting takes a glance in our direction
but there's no way she can know we're here.
When she turns back her face is difficult to read,
like making someone out in fog. We let the moment
pass, insofar as we have a say, and head
into the morning with our packs and loaded guns.

Hothouse

In the right context, *forever* can mean
anything. Completely out of context, it means *space*.
How do those houseplants know to grow that way?
How does my skin know to cool down?

I write a few words on my hand, including *balcony*
and *seeds*, then think about a torture that involves
shoots of bamboo. In my new notebook
I write *drown*, then on a new line

get me out of here. Light passes through
the roof and walls, absorbed into the earth
and all the contents of the room. How hot's
that terracotta get? How flexible's this

glass? I picture my veins bursting like an over
-pressured dam, pouring away, Old Testament red.
In my new notebook I write *Old Testament red*,
then on a new line *double doors*. I want my notes

to be a poem about the different kinds of pain –
loss of love, loss of loved one, etc. – but can't
decide on words to rhyme with *balcony*
or *drown*. Some of the trees

have been constrained so that they grow out
horizontally, their branches forced
down by a wire, which I learn later's called
espalier. One of the trees appears diseased,

its leaves dried out and turning brown,
like hair that changes white after a shock.
At home I start a poem I expect to call
'Espalier', about the different kinds of pain,

their uses, functions, methods, aims.
In the right context, forever *can mean / anything*,
it starts, the summer folding over itself,
a tropical vine weighed down by its fruits.

The Excavation

Then, a few years later, a man came in and slashed the canvas
with a knife. A statement was released that used the word *unbalanced*,
which seemed fair, although we hadn't had a statement from the slasher,
who was still detained. When we got home the furniture and wall-hangings
had gone. The paint behind the frames had not been faded by the light, so
left an outline of the pictures like a kind of silhouette. I felt surprisingly
disarmed, like being caught off guard without a good excuse, unable to
give answers to the simplest set of questions – *Who are you? What are you
doing here?* – suffering a period of brief but harsh amnesia. What better
metaphor than that great city, rising from the swamp, laying its
    foundations
on the men who died constructing it? It makes you wonder if survivors
had a clue what they'd survived, or if the long, fantastic stories told
by nurses did the trick. One inspector wrote how the drowned horses
were *impossible to count*, and that the bridges may as well have been
constructed out of them. The thing is, as a child, I didn't know how
distance worked, that it was somehow linked to passing time and that
forgetting sometimes meant that you might live through things again,
like when you feel you're seeing mountains that you've never seen
before but then you find out from a photograph you came here
not that long ago. About a year went by in the same way. For them,
there was a chance to fix up the slashed masterpiece, re-hanging
it beside a plaque explaining what had happened here. For us,
there was a chance to catch up on the things we'd missed, doing
our best to make exceptions for the minute gains and losses of each
day, which tend to sweep by unannounced the way the wind disturbs
acres of dunes. During this period we visited Lake Tahoe, which I'd only
ever seen as a relief map in a restaurant – whose outer walls were made
of plastic made to look like it was made of wood – or in *The Godfather: Part II*
(1974), because it's where the Corleones have a compound distanced
from New York. Driving north around the lake's perimeter, I read aloud
that its depth is over sixteen hundred feet and that (because the water
stays so cold) there could be bodies from the fifties down there,
perfectly preserved. Six yachts were sailing to the state line with their

fibreglass reflecting light. I had a vision stitched together from stock imagery of yachting scenes: mostly bikinis and champagne and people diving in slow motion from the yacht into the lake. It all got nasty pretty quickly, so I tried to think of something else. As far as I'm aware, though, this was years before the news broke out, by which time we were back at home. The papers barely covered other stories while the pictures started turning up on posters, T-shirts, flags and students' protest signs. Eventually the men came to be discharged from the hospital. It wasn't that they'd all been cured, just that there wasn't more that could be done; it would be years before the fossils were discovered and it all made sense.

REBECCA CULLEN

When you live in the same place nearly all your life, you develop ways of seeing the same things differently, but the past remains present. When I started writing, a cacophony of former selves demanded poems. Of these, 'Pillar Box Dress' is a contrary sonnet; 'North Sea' has a kind of wispy form, somewhere between memory and dream; '6 Brunswick Street' captures that time of freedom in the final year of a degree, revising in the garden with the future shimmering ahead.

After writing schemes of work, newsletters, briefs and all forms of forms, I wanted to choose what to write, deciding not to write about children or being a mother. This selection, though, reveals children with considerable expertise in hide and seek. 'Majid Sits in a Tree and Sings' was written after listening to a Libyan friend speak of the Gaddafi regime. Its short sentences break up the syntax, as though telling the whole story at once would be overwhelming. 'Crossing from Marazion' also focuses on an extraordinary child and mother.

'Opening' and 'Mother' were written while I was Poet in Residence at the ancestral home of George Gordon, Lord Byron, Newstead Abbey. It is a wild yet patterned place, and these poems also play with wildness and the pattern of repetition. 'Opening' was inspired by a pair of 200-year-old shoes and the mile-long Abbey driveway, its rhododendrons and ferns.

Several of this clutch of poems are very short, their length falling somewhere between a prayer and a 'news in brief' segment. In this context 'What I see in the Mirror' is a prayer of thanks for moisturising cream, 'The Courthouse, Shillelagh' is a report on the life of a circuit judge, and 'How to Hang Washing' is a meditation on finding pleasure in the commonplace.

Majid Sits in a Tree and Sings

This morning, I wake with a bird in my heart.
My mother smiles only for me. I bash my car into the wall.
Sometimes she tells me to be quiet. Today, she laughs.

The men came in the hottest part of the day.
A walk, my love, a small walk, she says.
In the stairwell, the mothers hold their children.

The guns shine in the sun. I am a man,
this is no time for play, I do not hide.
We shuffle in, look for a seat in the stands.

A big black bird comes down from the sky.
The grown-ups hold their breath. They are blinking a lot.
The bird likes the meat hanging on the goalposts.

Tonight, my mother says I can sleep in her bed.
I make my back into a curved shell against her legs.
She strokes her palm across my forehead.

In the middle of the night, I watch her on her knees.
She tips her head backwards. I see all of her neck.

Mother

Sometimes she is sick with new children, sometimes she is heavy with
    old ones.
Panels hide cupboards stuffed with capes and muffs, stacks of dove-grey
    boxes.
Panels hide balding dolls with wrists and ankles creased and fat. In a box,
there are boots with wooden soles for babies. There are boots for babies,
with wooden soles. The walls whisper things and promise. Her hands lie
    loose
in her lap. Lace droops on her arm. Her door is closed to queues of questions.
Her hands lie loose in her lap, when they should be busy blanketing or
    running.
Her cloth puckers at will, crumples; her palms are too hot, her fingers are
    too heavy.
On the table, a pair of silver bird scissors, a pair of gold-rimmed reading
    glasses.
There's a border she should be stitching, a border of a blue-winged fledgling.
Her hands lie loose in her lap. She slips out a child every year from under
    her skirts,
imagines every other baby crumpled in a brown paper bag. The walls
    whisper things
and promise. There are boots for babies with wooden soles. There's a border
she should be stitching. Her hands lie loose in her lap.

Opening

My shoes come sleeping in a box.
I hear them breathe inside the tissue-paper book,
the sound of rippling leaves.

The sole is thick alright, like a slab of black tripe;
the toes are tapered and stopped inside,
adding another inch – at least – in length.

Who knows I spade my feet? Kick trees
until the bark flakes, then blame the deer?
Who knows I use my shoes to root?

These are wild shoes
with points like noses, keen like foxes,
the leather creased like ears.

How to Hang Washing

It must be spring. There should be blackthorn
blossom, a smudge of sun across your cheek.

From your patch of earth, you'll hear the crest
of chatter from the playground at the school.

These pegs nip snugly, in time with magpie
calls, as your arms lift, stretch, clip, repeat.

What I See in the Mirror

A deep line that lags my face into a frown.
The way my cheeks sag, the loss of firm skin
around my mouth. My neck like a vacuum
cleaner pipe; a roosting place for flocks
of chins. In my small sharp eyes, brimming
with the undertow, the clarity of rage.
I make sounds like laughter, slightly louder
and more hearty; scoop hope out of a jar,
apply a thick layer, nightly.

Midas

Your sigh is salt escaping from a cellar.
You watch the girl with grazes on her knees.

You are a forest of hands, a nuisance
in a clearing, stammering a sorry.

You want the girl to think of you and smile, to be the sand
she finds in the toe of her shoe long after a holiday.
As it is, you're having trouble getting her to understand
your particular kind of sign language.

6 Brunswick Street

Every afternoon now, we hear the clock
ticking down through next door's window.
We've pulled the sofa outside, our chairs
and cups. *Bring on the books*, we shout;
John steps out with Beckett on his head.
We are speaking other people's words,
practising our bows. We are cramming
three years into our skulls, already
brimming with ourselves. One of Paul's
shoes is in the corner. He's lost the other;
it doesn't matter. We've been sunning
ourselves all May, all June. Barely clean,
completely looking, no one wearing shades.

Pillar Box Dress

I come to you with no hope in my knees. We sit,
make the pub a confessional. Condensation slips
down the outside of my glass. We're here again:
same date, same table, same dress. Bonfire night
runs in the background, like a television on mute
during tea. We're talking in shrapnel. By the time
my drink is gone, your brother's waiting at the bar.
You say something about a spark. I stand, go home.

I don't leave drunken messages on your phone.
I play that song you never liked and sleep sprawled
across the bed. I keep my head. This much I know:
I'll change my hair, you'll be back by the New Year.
You're with the girl whose pout reminds you of Lolita.
In the morning, I fold the red dress and post it to her.

The Courthouse, Shillelagh

In the gardens, a shack no longer full of glass,
but restored to the small courthouse it once was,
pocks in the wood where the judge's ring hit the lid,
faced with plaintiff and perpetrator. A man of tweed
and stout boots, travelling the countryside settling disputes
over the primogeniture of a bull, a badly-tailored suit,
a grasped boundary or unreturned long-promised favour.
Still the rain comes, the common denominator.

Orlando

after Kim Moore

I was dry mouthed in the Coliseum while you faced
the lions, and we read Classics and punted, and foiled
the mob and kept the diamonds. I wore your shoes
although they were too small for me, was your amanuensis,
and we owned a sweet shop, and a bookshop, and you were
the book I took out and kept, then lent and never got back.
We lived in frames opposite each other in the long gallery,
my breeches were plum velvet and you wore a clove
orange round your wrist, and we ached from quaffing
sherbet, and hid in the hollow of a tree. We were ravishing
on chaise longues brandishing gold-tipped cigarettes,
and hoofers drying out our stockings over the bath,
and boarders, in the same dorm, floating on our backs
after a midnight feast, in a natural pool filled by the tide.

Crossing from Marazion

I am six when people first begin to stare –
a boy in man's clothing,
children leaping in my footsteps,
kite-tailing across the beach.

The mothers stand in doorways, trill
He must wear his father's shoes!
What height will he reach full grown?
We leave a single track.

At ten I anchor the village team
at tug of war. Then I join father
on the boat, learn to haul creels,
he says I am worth three men to him.

The Whit Fair waltzes in
with whispers of the Show of Freaks.
The catch is bad. There is a curse.
My father's jaw sets firm.

That night, I see mother trawl her brow.
At low tide, she takes my hand and we walk the causeway to the friars.

North Sea

You stood on my mat in your muddy boots,
tilting your chin like a dare.

For two weeks I pined. I was a beach for sweating horses,
woke with hoof prints on my hands.

We played ourselves with a bow made from the fine tail-hair
of a horse running across a beach.

In the morning, I was shy of the creature you had made,
velvet in my ear.

VALA THORODDS

Sometimes I think that everything I know about poetry I learned from music – that my poetic education was in fact musical. Growing up I admired my mother's brothers, who played and sang classical music. I went to a lot of their concerts, saw a lot of operas; sat and watched and listened, as much at intermission as during the performances, and learned about pauses – about the spaces between events, people, notes, breaths. My first love, inconceivably, inevitably, was disco. For years I wanted to be a dancer, and I practised every kind of dance I could find, until puberty hit and I started rowing – that tremendous, meditative dance on water.

The central concern here is transcendence – and my hope is to evoke, in my poems, the feeling of listening to music or losing oneself in the rhythm of movement. Poetry can do this while accommodating the intellect. If what happens in the mind can be felt as intensely as what happens in the body – if we can, in fact, orgasm in our sleep – then poetry is, whatever else it is, the mind's way of dancing.

These poems are concerned with how bodies measure time. They look at the ways in which we are inhabited, but they also seek to inhabit. The spirit dwells in us like a curse or a spell, and these poems try to embody that haunted feeling. Perhaps they seek also to be an incantation themselves, to disarm and entrance like music.

Enemies

Beyond the reach of the body
            – we insist.

Balance our submission,
coarse and delicate. Spoil
the thing to get closer
to the thing.

           Afterwards
kneeling. Gentle. Ask
for the exception, beg to see
the sight seen only with eyes
closed.

Reciprocity
is a soft animal.

Attempting to satisfy,
your boastful display
of contempt.

Down the leaves.
Wet the dry. The way
takes only a moment.

We are sharper than words
and steeper.

Through Flight

For a moment
we are borne into the air
and then down.

It is there, behind everything.

On the corner outside your *Wohnung*
where the steps descend
to meet the train
you leave,
it stops.

What is rawness but an opening?

The space inside me to which you climb
and never leave.

Four hours, ours
then I begin counting down.
(What a long journey this life will be
without you.)

Meanwhile the train slips through the night
and we hear nothing. Past the place we inhabited
on different strata, unseeing.

Until evening, the air calm
after a day of enveloping everyone.

And it's just us. The stove. The coffee
has done heating. Smoke
out of the window. It is us. Just.

Inertia

Not lack of movement, but a steadying
between bodies.

I wake to find the things I couldn't say in the dream.

The space between train and platform
like the space between this night and the last

where you wait with ink-stained fingers,
water-stained mouth.

Between us, an interval
that separates now from the canal.

It's not the distance
between here and there
that is unbridgeable.

We live this moment across years.

The pull between planets
that near but never meet.

The Difference

Always a second or two longer than you think.
Not long, but long
considering.

(Because)
breaths, almost,
are the seconds after
when the body comprehends
what the mind can't concede.

Trying to remember

(something about April)

those gasps

Naked except for the jewellery

You sketched a shelf
for all your imaginary things. Plants and records.
Outlines of books that exist only in your future, best life.

Offered to add something of mine, whatever I liked.

But I couldn't think
of what I cared for. So I said, 'Jewellery.'
'Sweaters and shoes.'

When I meant, 'My bike lock.'
'Procrastination.'
'The lies I told.'

in

touching
the periphery
excited, finally
about something beyond the real

(what happens with the body
always being like a secret
we carry within)

the light of morning draws lines
hinting at the shapes of things outside

as in the dream
where your mother
is not your mother

the face not hers
but breasts
insinuating
and tongue

anticipation grows
out of everything

desire burrows outward
from shadow
brutal, clean as a mirror

Rain

She came at night
heavy in the dark

at the window, she looked
divine.

Answered,
I'm *whispering*.

Holy

Holy

Holy

whispers.

Antidotes to the ghosts.

Pressed against the pane,
hungry for kisses,
they offer up your memory.

This is what it is about.
Your body in some room and you are no longer there.

We rush forward.
Past the edge.
Not yet.

We are almost there.

Luck

Hard to imagine, two moments
possible at once.

Amid the terror, bliss.

While the rest were made to wade
blood, we made quiet.
Swept it through y-
our visible
exquisite
trans-
lucent veins.

Tonight,
as it happens,
and again tomorrow,
only different.
Then we are allowed morning.

Our hushed breath
granted / taken.

Carelessly we have entangled ourselves

and any unravelling
will be just that –
an unsympathetic tug
and tearing
and tearing
and of course
we know this.

I don't know how
but somehow
it's all of this
stuff,
here in this bag,
with all the coins just
lying there
at the bottom, exposed.

I hate change,
but you are easy in a way I never will be,
taking a big sip of water as if it were the source
of your actual
perfect health.

It is your body
that is at your surface,
you lucky dog; you are exhilarated
by the things put here
to sustain you
and if you were an animal,
actually, you would be this horse
we are passing on our way home,
content with the utter simplicity of this grass
and this wind

and soon a firm smoothing with my palm
of all the hairs
on the back of your neck.

I am terrified
that I am the bird
that lands on you for a moment
and when I breathe
you feel my whole body shaking
with the effort of being alive.

I am about you
in circles
obsessed
for that tiny bug
that specific
seed
and you are
meanwhile
just there
capable and magnanimous
drinking the water as if it were the obvious
happiness.

Here it comes now, my
hundredth
sip of air
for your one,

my bones full of it
barely there
but singing
on the inhale
Of course, my horse,
of course.

Aperture

Pressed against the glass
the boys see only the moon
reflected cold
bright
and white.

It's the fear that gets closer

and the hands.

The itching that makes it the same.

Virgins white as whales,
as virgins, raw as film
developing under the night sky, slowly.

We see only fingerprints.

Our secrets concealed by light
and our hands sticky
from the sugar of things.

LISA KELLY

The other day I asked my daughter, 'Can you pass me the thing that opens the door?' The word *key* having eluded me. The idea of fluency interests me – and whether we can ever claim fluency in any language. Words and articulacy are power, but words escape me all the time; not only words that I can't recall or names I've forgotten but words I mishear or miss altogether because of my deafness in my left ear. Also, listening to my mother speaking Danish for two weeks every year when my grandparents visited from Copenhagen was fascinating, yet alienating as I couldn't understand my mother's tongue. Three members of my family suffered with dementia and journeyed from fluency to the ultimate inarticulacy. To what extent language builds or diminishes identity is a preoccupation. How Danish am I, not speaking Danish? How Deaf am I with my clumsy attempts at British Sign Language? I have to work hard to listen and this requires me to place you to my right side, to watch your lips, to watch your hands, to watch your gestures. How can form not matter? To understand what you say, I must attempt to control our interrelated physical space. Of course, I often fail and confusion, mis-interpretation and annoyance, as well as humour, are by-products. My poems reflect my obsession with form and the physical space that words occupy on the page. Attempting to 'hang onto' sound means aids, such as rhyme, are appreciated. Escaping from noise into silence and reading means lines, phrases and fragments from books are often more keenly heard than what is being said to me in everyday life. However, language is as much visual as it is aural. I am excited by the appearance of words, their material quality and the condensed narratives of names. Working as a freelance journalist specialising in technology gives me a level of fluency in esoteric acronyms and a specialist language which masks technophobia. Alternative perceptions offer a relief from the tyranny of pseudo-articulacy. Only politicians' speeches pretend otherwise. The multiplicity and multifariousness of language, communication and understanding means every interpretation is possible, and possibly wrong. But some fun and perhaps progress towards empathy can be had playing with these ideas along the way.

Apple Quartet

I. JAUNE DE METZ

Repeat *If you love me, pop and fly. If you hate me,*
burn and die, and think of your amour as you cast
a pip in the fire. At my ripe age, I look on wildings

with a jaundiced eye. Once skin was golden
like the future. Fortune is a liar. He the scion
of a rich family, I from strong stock. Such notions

of choice; in the hearth, a pip scorched desire. No ladders
to reach an apple hanging like a heart in hock. I grafted,
kept close to the earth, was nothing to birdsong,

good breeding in every branch to which pickers
would flock. My crown not high enough for sheep
to graze beneath, among village gossip, wisdom of

soil and season, gatherings to celebrate harvest
with cider and song. *Old apple tree we wassail thee*
superseded by reason. Longing for lanterns, ribbons

to tie around limbs betrayed by the aphid's
white ruff of treason. What auguries in peel
can the earth descry? *If you hate me, burn and die.*

II. THE APPLE MACHINE

Where worms, roots and fingers
mesh, the future is buried in an apple
machine: Redlove sliced

for ruddy flesh. No dwarfing rootstock
helped the queen control the apple
that blessed the bough. A poisoned mind

finds time to dream. Dwarfs mined mountains
for rubies – now *Malling 9* is paradise
preserved. We scatter before we plough,

discard the fruit that isn't curved
to mimic the perfect orb of the sun;
a diamond bite cosmetically preferred

by queens, kings, everyone. A tooth
puller in a souk in Marrakesh wields
pliers to pluck what fireblight

has undone. Like a princess we sleep
in the machine's crèche where worms,
roots and fingers mesh.

III. HERE, APPLE TREE

Here, branches are stark against white
sky, their bronchial diagram a lesson in
breath. A snared plastic bag puffs with

effort to fly free of some small death,
empty of exotic fruit carried
from shelves, the carrier holds its own

trashed shibboleth. Here, custom rots slower
than our apple selves, rosy at the
buffet, all you can eat for the price of burst

buttons, girdles, belts loosening
at the heart's abnormal beat to a defibrillation
rhythm, a wassail haunting the wind

in clamour for retreat from acres
of sterilised soil. Half-recalled, *If you hate
me burn and die*, blown fireblight,

an orange sun's broil. On the out-breath,
If you love me, pop and fly. Here,
branches are white against stark sky.

IV. *A IS FOR APPLE*

Abbot's Early, Ashmead's Kernel, Autumn Pearmain
Barchard's Seedling, Billy Down Pippin, Bloody Butcher
Cap of Liberty, Carswell's Honeydew, Cummy Norman

Doctor Clifford, Dog's Snout, Duke of Devonshire
Early Bower, Easter Orange, Eccleston Pippin
Fair Maid of Taunton, Falstaff, Forest Styre

George Carpenter, Gillyflower of Gloucester, Gin
Hall Door, Hangydown, Hope Cottage Seedling
Improved Woodbine, Irish Peach, Iron Pin

Jackets and Waistcoats, Jo Jo's Delight, Jordan's Weeping
Keed's Cottage, Kernel Underleaf, Kingston Black
Leathercoat Russet, Lemon Queen, Lucombe's Seedling

Macfree, Marston Scarlett Wonder, Merton Prolific
Nancy Jackson, Netherton Late Blower, Neverblight
Oaken Pippin, Old Cornish Cooker, Onion Redstreak

Painted Summer Pippin, Palmer's Rosey, Pam's Delight
Quarren Dow, Quarry, Queen Caroline
Racky Down, Radford Beauty, Rathe Ripe

Slack-ma-Girdle, Snell's Glass Apple, Sops-in-Wine
The Rattler, Tinsely Quince, Tower of Glamis
Underwood Pippin, Upright French, Upton Pyne

Vagnon Archer, Valentine, Vallis
Wardington Seedling, Warrior, Wealthy
Excel Jonagold, Excelsior, Exeter Cross

Yarlington Mill, Ye Old Peasgood, Yellow Ingestrie
Yeovil Sour, Yorkshire Aromatic, Zari.

Trailing Spouse

Near the pool, I picked a frangipani blossom.
By the time I spoke to the maid, its petal edges
were breakfast-cereal brown.

Everything is either overripe or sticky –
mangoes, rice, my thighs. Except the maid.
A silk dress would slip and pool at her ankles.

Like the Pomeranian, the baby must be paraded
every day at least twice on the little patch
of grass with all the other babies and Pomeranians.

Work. The Mall. Both are air-conditioned.
Both colonise time. There are compensations,
but like the breeze, they are mostly offshore.

Battling for their place under the ceiling light,
the moths are migraine-inducing. We drink
imported wine. She doesn't want sex.

Whitewash

The faded swastika on the side of the barn
is showing through the latest layer of paint
and must be painted over by the owner again.

Our generation is generous it seems.
Over dinner we discuss how the farmer's daughter
was a victim of her beautiful genes,

no choice but to take the Nazi officer's seed.
'What would you do?' The sort of moral dilemma
sorted over a second bottle, until resentment breeds.

Your great uncle *a prêté serment* –
swore an oath to Pétain – and was *préfet*
of Calvados. I translate this to an easy life in Caen.

I ask if, after the war, he was detained.
You say, *surveillance gardée*, (is there a difference?)
but his possessions and farm were returned.

I boast of my Danish uncle who fought in the resistance.
You stress yours was an uncle *only* by marriage.
Where is this going? Nowhere, but we are persistent,

stripping off layers of skin to expose raw nerves,
find iron in blood, the cross in the ribcage –
what of us that shows through, what it proves

Out of Order

You say a sign should hang from my ear,
you say torture with Chinese Whispers,
like the door on the toilet refusing to flush.
I'll say whatever comes into my ear as shush.
I say there is no blockage, no glue or wax,
you'll accuse me of negative feedback,
just nerves dead as disconnected wires.
I say thank God for books, my ear retires,
you say playing with a rotary phone
far from the playground's monotone,
picking up the receiver to my good ear,
you say you'll get me in the mere –
bad: dial tone/no dial tone, is wacko.
Oh-noes playing Marco Polo,
I say I'm testing how to differentiate
a unilateral ear unable to locate
between fitting in/not fitting in.
Oi! Are you deaf or something?

A Map Towards Fluency

I. BEDROCK

I map *a*————————————to my left thumb
Alex maps *a*————————————to his right thumb
e————————————to my left forefinger
poor Alex, the teacher can't map sinistral————to dextral
thesaurus maps sinistral————————to sinister
a hammer mapped a red line————to his drummer's hand

i————————————to my left middle finger
(Sophie maps *i*————————to her *swear finger*)

o————————————to the gold of my ring finger
u————————————to my left pinkie

map a twist of fist in the gut————————to hate
a raised pinkie thrust forward————————to bad
an open palm on the heart————————to like

finger men meet————————————to greet

hands beckon a welcome————————at waist level
the weight of weather————————at the altitude of cheekbones

Helena, who can't remember the palm-to-palm swish of her capital H
marks each digit with a marker pen————————*a*
————————————*e*
————————————*i*
————————————*o*
————————————*u*

(is this cheating?)

Words are shifting animals
                    a fish is a handshimmer
                                a bird, a forefinger beaking a thumb
a cat is claws, preening whiskers

Colours clothe the body in a flash of flesh

Red *brushes* lips   Blue *strokes* back of hand
Green *grazes* forearm   Black *knuckles* cheek
Pink *taps* nose   White *flares* fingers

What has happened to Alex?
                    Helena has changed her shift, and is here
Late from an audition, Sophie circles sorry at the centre of her chest, her
    cheeks
a tapped nose

We bring our colours and animals with us

    Helena, a forefinger beaking thumb, settles on the edge of her chair
    Alex, an absent handshimmer

III. OUTCROP

Jean
our teacher
is a landmark
All eyes look to her
What can you see out of your
peripheral vision? Furrows forming
and reforming on ever more familiar faces
Gestures formed and reformed by ever more
familiar hands: rings, scars, tattoos. We keep our
distance. Eyes cannot whisper. Air, larynx, tongue:
all fingers and thumbs. As a child, Jean was forced to
sit on her hands. *Don't point! Don't touch!* Now her hands
guide us towards an alternative view. She signs, we are touched

IV. PRECIOUS MINERALS

Context is everything

We are unearthing

the philosopher's stone

Base metal can be turned into   a fist
on a fist
flexing into splayed fingers

Bank is   a fist with thumb cocked, stamping the palm
Aid is ·   a fist with thumb up, proffered on the palm

How old?   fingers dance on the nose
How much?   fingers dance on the chin

Alex is in   a heavy metal band

On a world tour without him, it is laughing all the way to
                              the fist with thumb cocked, stamping the palm

Helena's fingers dance on her chin

On a world tour without him, it cannot offer
                              a fist with thumb up, proffered on the palm

Alex says he is feeling his age

Sophie's fingers dance on her nose

V. EROSION

I imagine our hands chopped off as Philomela had her tongue cut out
What would there be to say? How would we say it?
Not able to weave our stories into a tapestry
Alex unable to drum his rhythm. Sophie
unable to sign her song. Helena
unable to recall her felt-tipped
fingers. Alex laughs, which
is how it should be
We are going our
separate ways
towards fluency
and erosion
The future
a hand thrust
forward
the past
a wave
over the
shoulder

A Desultory Day

It's the sort of day with spit but no polish,
the sort of day when a neighbour makes hay
with my husband's amiable manner
and extracts a *maybe* to sort out her fruit trees.
It's the sort of day you say, It's *that sort of day*
to help you get through. It's the sort of day
I fall in love with a Japanese man
for the way he stands magnificently
in his trunks while his daughters play croquet.
It's the sort of day a towel serves
as a skirt, and a jumper as a headscarf,
the sort of day eyes jump from horse rider
to horse rider in the bay. It's the sort of day
a father drags a pram across the sand backwards,
the sort of day a fat baby tries to catch
fat feet, the sort of day when not just thoughts stray.

The Dogs of Pénestin

Argos,[1] Hound,[2] Banga,[3] Lassie,[4]
Son-of-George,[5] Bear,[6] Snowy,[7]

Fang,[8] Gyp,[9] Old Yeller,[10] Toto,[11]
Böwser vön Überdog,[12] Sorry-oo,[13]

Cadpig, Lucky, Roly Poly, Patch,[14]
Pearl the Wonder Dog,[15] Ponch,[16]

Crab,[17] Frank the Pug,[18] Skulker,[19]
Bull's-eye,[20] K9,[21] John Joiner,[22]

Prince Amir of Kinjan,[23] Wellington,[24]
Hong Kong Phooey,[25] Gai-Luron,[26]

Sirius,[27]
Cerebrus.[28]

1. Waits by the gate for his mistress, in Syria with Médecins Sans Frontières.
2. Destroyed for leaving gigantic, muddy footprints.
3. His master is a Pilates instructor, partial to a Margarita cocktail.
4. Rescued a young boy from the sea at Loscolo.
5. Sheep worrier, hated by Brécean farmer Gabriele Chêne.
6. Chocolate Labrador belonging to Luka who also has a bear called Dog.
7. An adventurous wire-fox terrier regularly walked by a failed abstract artist.
8. Belongs to the seven-foot-six gamekeeper of Le Lesté.
9. Trots at the heels of his carpenter master.
10. Enjoys wild boar hunts with Travis Manteaux.
11. Penchant for chewing his mistress's red slippers.
12. A vicious bulldog; detests the llamas from Cirque Medrano.
13. Howls at the moon and dreams of his wolf brothers in Brocéliande.
14. Puppies owned by Cruella de la Ville, a supporter of Marine Le Pen.
15. German Shorthaired Pointer, a couch-potato pooch.
16. Appears to live in some sort of squirrel universe.
17. Described by his incontinent master as a cruel-hearted cur.
18. Owned by a policeman who claims he can talk.
19. Huge, purple tongue hangs half a foot out of his mouth.
20. A white shaggy dog, with his face scratched and torn in twenty different places.
21. Bark has a metallic ring. His master, Dr Qui, collects watches.
22. Saved a kitten from being eaten by two giant rats.
23. Afghan Hound puppy that makes a mess on the cliff paths.
24. Poodle involved in a gardening accident.
25. Belongs to a mild-mannered janitor who dabbles in martial arts.
26. Melancholic Basset Hound from the same litter as Droopy.
27. Heavenly dog worshipped by all the other dogs of Pénestin.
28. No one who enters his property, Enfer, is seen coming out alive.

Anonymous

after the New Yorker cartoon by Peter Steiner, 1993

On the internet, nobody knew I was a dog,
how I'd raise my hind leg to piss, bark
viciously at cats on my anonymous blog.

O trolls, those dog days were a lark.
I, Sirius, outshone all in the Canis Major,
blew my master's whistle in his park.

Bitch! he yelled. *Track and cage her.*
Failed to guess at my dog's bollocks,
as I buried my bone-to-pick deeper

in the Darknet where encryption locks.
Once bitten, twice bitcoin:
a silken road to Anything Stocked.

Second lifer, don't whimper – feign
identities. Dangle spam bait, flog
lives as authorities neuter the anodyne.

Only saps are hacked as they iSlog.
On the internet, nobody knows I am a dog.

A Chorus of Jacks in 13 Texts

after Porphyria

UR t% BUTful 4 yor Lyf 2 nd happily, t% BUTful 4 a closing shot of yor
fAc :-) in2 a soapy sunset

We knew he'd b a cad, wear u lIk arm candy, reveal intimacies Ovr
cards f he c%d plA NEthing mo sophisticated thN >@< Crush

He mA L%k lIk a Victorian gentleman, w Hs moustache & side-burns,
bt he's a digital darling, kEpn Hs connections OpN

U wer born out of era. aL yor letters shud b RitN on violet paper, scented
w violet water, sealed w a violet :-*

insted UR forced 2 sext DIS vile man, endure Hs violent demands 4 <)
& beer, Hs insistence dat tap H2O iz BetA 2 bathe n thN bubLE

We hav Hs number, we hav aL Hs on9 accounts hacked. d 3:o) he
met Bhind yor beautifully-boned bak iz not evN an on9 comment, a
Facebook Like, retweet, not evN hEr

Don't wori we wud not harm a hair on yor hed cuz U L%k aftR yor
hair, & she didn't. It wz tied bak w a rubR band, & itz casualness wz
unbearable

2 tink how he wound dat rat tail rownd Hs fingers wen dey kissed,
whIl U sat aloN by d window, yor tresses holdN d moon's gleam

2 tink dat makes us cry & so she had 2 cry too, 2 knO how much it hrtz
2 luv U lIk we do

4giv us 4 bn soppy, bt U mAk us sentimental, mAk us txt things we
shouldn't, mAk us flame, mAk us troll

Really, it's yor fault. f it wz not 4 yor yeLo hair, yor smooth white sholdR bare, we wud not hav 2 luv U lIk we do, not hav 2 foLow U on Instagram

foLow U om, let ourselves in2 yor basement w d key code texted 2 d cad, hu won't b comin, won't eva b comin anywhere eva agen

W8 2 presnt U w aL her hair n 1 lng yeLo string az a token of our tragic luv

Cuddles are Drying up Like the Sun in a Data Lake

Sun is such a hard word, like a boiled sweet
in one of those round travel sweet tins
that nobody wants unless they're sick,
those citrus colours: lemon, lime and orange
that even without tasting make your mouth water
to counter the churn in your stomach.

Sun is such a hard word, with its 's' and 'n'
that could have an 'o' or an 'i' slotted between
for that Donnian pun or a postlapsarian chime
making it harder to give birth to or acknowledge,
spat out in a sibilant spray of spittle
ending in bright, shining negation.

Sun is such a hard word, once part of Microsystems
swallowed by Oracle, its SPARC processor in LEON
designed for space use, a fully open-source
implementation that neither you nor I
can understand, the most likely meaning:
cuddles are drying up like the sun in a data lake.

Ladybird

Every autumn I forget they do this,
until they do –
hard-faced carapaces,
little mechanical legs
across my bedroom ceiling
insinuating into warm gaps,

congregating under cornices,
black-eyed blotches staring me down.

Ladybird, ladybird fly away home
Your house is on fire, and your children are gone

Occasionally, a maverick, lured by the mellow glow
of the bedside light, will lift its elytra,
like the doors on a Lamborghini
to reveal filmy black wings,

and fly towards my open mouth.

Ladybird, lazy bird fly out of bed
Your home is infested ...

but I shrink back from scooping its crunchiness
into tissue, messing
with its reflex bleeding, yellow toxins oozing
out of its exoskeleton.

All except one and that's little Ann

(The receptionist had a tattoo on her arm.
In its freckled baby belly, *Always in my heart*)

For she crept under the frying pan
For she crept under the counterpane

Aphid Reproduction as Unpunctuated White Noise

.

a full stop is an aphid not a comma nor an embryo
an aphid is a full stop is a nymph not a womb holding
a comma nor a question mark asks nothing of a slash
or a backslash bulges with parentheses bears
afterthought after afterthought as a full stop
parthenogenetic filled with full stops without
stopping without comma without pausing full stop
after full stop never comma not a comma until
all the space is taken with full stop upon full stop
not a comma and a full stop develops wings flies off

!

an exclamation mark is an aphid on the wing not a
full stop not a comma nor an embryo an aphid is
an exclamation mark not a womb holding a comma
nor a question mark asks nothing of a slash or a
backslash bulges with parentheses bears afterthought
after afterthought as a full stop parthenogenetic
not an exclamation mark not a comma but a full stop
filled with exclamation marks filled with full stops
bears exclamation marks filled with full stops
until summer heat has happened and love is in the air

.

an aphid is a male on the wing not a full stop
is an exclamation mark and an aphid is a female
on the wing not a full stop is an exclamation mark
gives birth to a full stop without wings mates

LISA KELLY 269

with an exclamation mark and lays a full stop
a full stop is an egg not an aphid but an egg
and the egg it is dormant is a full stop not a pause
not a comma nor an embryo but a full stop in the winter
without wings an egg is a full stop until spring
and it hatches a full stop is an aphid not a full stop

ANDREW LATIMER

Most, if not all, of the poems included here were written whilst working in a supermarket bakery. The routine – the early starts, followed by equally early finishes – was conducive to writing poetry. In particular, the twelve- and fourteen-line, rhetorical short poem. This sonnet*ish* poem, with its volta acting as dynamo – propelling and organising – makes its material memorable just long enough until it can be scribbled down – during a lunch break or stolen toilet stop.

Here are just eight examples. Their settings range between tenth-century Japan, early twentieth-century Antarctica, paper-thin medieval backdrops and Melanesian cannibal tribes. There are homages to Andrew Marvell, Marriane Moore, Bink Noll, as well as a chorus of anonymous Latin and medieval writers.

The Poet in the Garden

The poet in the garden counts the shoots
like syllables, the vegetable language
slowly forms. Sibyl in a bamboo cage
contorts the meaning in the scattered fruits.

Every thought is an attack on nothing,
a forage for the hedgerow deity.
Words abound but do not bite their meaning;
the blue tit waits, prepared for longer play.

Then memory, like a hard rime, returns,
says go in fear of the organic form.
The garden disappears inside the worm
and the poet, spat out, is forced to leave.

Parts of the feast remain – tuber and blooms.
Thoughts into words harden – tight little tombs.

from Scott's Journals

Saturday; at Camp, I scattered some oats.
Weary Willy has kept the course so far
and the ponies seem to be strong. The clouds
are thin and rolling in Antarctic pink.
Saw James Pigg, Michael and Snatcher up ahead
and we drew up within an hour to rest.
The men are pink and soft and kind in chaff
and laugh between the quiet creaking ice.

At Shambles Camp we gave ourselves some sleep,
the snow like sand, loose upon the surface,
holds us back as the seasons hurry on.
We had our best hoosh yet – a pemmican
horse-meat stew which really heats the belly.
Canzone, I' sento gia stancar la penna.

from The Pillow Book of Sei Shōnagon

An earthen cup
          an ill woman in the eyes of her lover
a torn-up letter put together again
          the inside of a cat's ear

the mayfly and the firefly
          priests. fruit. horses as well as oxen
silver tweezers that still pluck the hair
          women of the lower classes

paradise
on an old man's back
the sound of comb-teeth snapping

the seventh month
(when it is cool) reading
these lines in another girl's notebook.

The Musician

A Sketch of John Dowland in Denmark

Through pipes and contraptions
I come to you,
from a cellared world
my angular intention

aspires. What's hellish is
hidden.
Only the beauty
survives.

Through distance and exile
I came to you,
and wormed my way into the

core. Once insidious, now
ridiculous, singing
through pipes and contraptions.

Pavane: Anubis

I give the green-fruit,
try for transcendence,

        these the gifts, this the dance,
        those the people believing.

I, long as corn,
jackal-headed corn,

        scale the heart, feed the dogs,
        those the people believing.

Thin limbs
      with skirt and flail
           foot following flute.

The dancers part
      ethic and image,
           those the people believing.

A Medieval Scene

The clack of the carriage chasing the bell's
chirrup.
        The burning urge to arrest smells
                on the page.
The mirror within an inch of the eye.

      Kick me!
if ever I disappoint the image
or break the *sabbatizare*.
         I am clearly
an apple on the slow-moving ass's
back. Drawn up the hill / whatever pleases.

The clack of the trap chasing the ass moves
me as I think it should move you. These grooves

in the hillside / signs of our obedience.

Mi Donna é Prega

A lady is pregnant, so I must sing
of some wild passion, the saleable type,
love straight as a needle, blunt at the tip,
an accident, and a well-plotted thing.
It grows from the damaged area,
the bit behind the eyes, where thoughts reside,
it is, despite belief, a parasite:
devours reason, exudes hysteria,
you remember what you have never known,
a crimson cloth, a sentimental song,
it spreads its choler along the phloem
causing men to bark, when they mean to sing.
There is no cure, but it can show mercy –
infect another, or kill you quickly.

Jamshid

Invented much, saw much more invented,
watched the marrow bloat, and peopled the land.
Fit of form, never one to catch a cold,
and got the wine, almost all, into the bowl.
Did learn the way before the what, the how
rather than the why, seeing they'd given
me more time than one could ask for – rocks
to sand, and having outdone the earth went
onto the sea.
                  Have taken orders from
no man, nor a god. Felt just what could touch,
brine in the cut lip, the wind's embrace. Then,
if needed, bred. So have passed three hundred
years.

Matthew

We say the same things but do not always
Agree; argue with words until out of
Line. Someone must decide what comes and what
Goes; take the axe towards the lyric tree.

Light, swift as a cow's tail across its rump,
Came. Said I. Beckoned me go, who was gold,
Gathering rust in a small back-end town.

That was it. Exactly as each word fell.
And the shortest. *Meek*. Made the loudest bang.

The manifold sound of that ringing out
We cannot agree on. How long on each?

Someone should go and put an end to it.

Sant Iago

Credulous mollusc-man, who knew the price
of travel. That it is better to be
somewhere else. Better to have hat and stick,
than wife and kids. Better, even, to have
blisters. We cannot all be masters. One
should follow, trailing behind with the thieves
and rams. But what a scoop of life it is!

Perhaps, while stopped, in the ochre valleys
at Villamajor, or Ciraqui,
you saw in the sky his gathering house,
the tragic loading of his tragic bed,
and knew that walking could not get you there?

Cleopatra Playing Boules

Most Sweet Queen –
No more music, the false maker of mood.
Those in love are poisoned by the general
tongue, singing with a century's sickness
not their own. Rather Play! Roll the moment
on towards the crisp, cut grass of England,
and breathless, sucking peaches, roll again.
                              How now, Lady!
Man is the maker, so woman makes joy
in breaking up his boring constancy.
                              Hear me, Queen.
First, see the playing green swell with laughter
beneath our game. It rolls itself below
the balls and makes no time for history.

White & Manila

for Bink Noll

Your package was not delivered
Because there was no one at home;
We tried to force the window but
Failed, and merely upset the cat.
A second attempt was made, but
When we called at your door you were
Searching ferociously for keys,
And seemed unworthy of the gift.
Your package was not delivered
A third time because we opened it
Ourselves and enjoyed its bright
Entrails hungrily (whilst sorting boys
Swooped around our heads like vultures).

We have delivered over two thousand
Packages this year without fail,
But not yours. Perhaps
This is due to some fault at the root
Of your character, or something
Unresolved in the tangled
Ecology of your family tree.
Nevertheless, we will endeavour
To call at the threshold of your house
Each day, and hand over a thick packet
Of white and manila notices.

from Seneca the Younger

Spring kills the old man in his sleep, sucks out
the marrow and buries the bones. Will you
doze even when you feel it approaching?

Your dead mass will sprout in the green pillage
of spring. It demands a sacrifice. Half-
way into elm-bark, out of her old skin,
Daphne wants winter. Much still to be done.

The season decides, the climate dictates
the outcome. You will lose a lot
in the process. After the last green surge

you will look for yourself and probably
not find it. Then you will try to speak and...

your voice will be first to go
and then your good looks, but who will notice?

Head-Hunting

If you aren't in over your head, how do you know how tall you are?

Some eat of the body, having the head
safely removed. I do not. There is food
enough in the jungle and there is bread.
Nor do I drink of the blood.

The mask-makers have discarded the host,
filleting the flesh instead of steaming
the bone. The old methods are quickly lost;
they cannot hear their ancestors screaming.

Time passes. It swallows the nights and spits
out the days. My sons are old. One is calm
and the other, of course, is full of knots.
His soul is grasping for the higher palm.

They call me Lazarus, because I talk
of the dead as if I knew them. They hunt
and bring back head-names for the little folk.
My thoughts are long rivers, my knife is blunt.

We drum our songs, get on with the neighbours,
such peace has been very hard to come by.
A wind dies amongst the trees, and the boars
sound like hunters advancing up the Fly

River. The snapping of the spine is like
bamboo breaking: there is the crunch and then
the liquid ripping of tendons. We woke
to find the caustic dance done, our women

siphoned from us. As a boy you must learn
the hierarchy of the parts: a foot
counts for nothing on its own, a jawbone
is better, but a head is the real loot.

We hunt the bird for its ecstatic plume,
the rhino its horn, the monkey its tail.
We seek the things our bodies can't assume,
man attacks man for his rational.

Into gardens, behind low-pitched houses,
a migrant peace finds another village,
sits down to spell out its vowelled stories.
Outside, the world is on a different page.

How wide they dream, the unforgivable!
plucking out their words as if they had no
muddy root, stretching their pliable
meanings like hunters stringing their bows.

The dreamer half-tormented, half-inspired,
throws a rope to his imagination,
hoping to tie it down to fact. The tired
dreamer, full of knots, that one is my son.

He shakes the room with his upfacing palms,
the men around him vigorously nod.
The talk of revenge breeds eager lambs,
quick to unite, quicker to make a god.

Over the cool grass my feet go, thinking
of where I have been. There are no tracks
that lead to this point, the earth has eaten
them hungrily. For this there are no maps.

I heard his voice, walking in the garden,
and rushing in I clenched all time at once.
He is calm. On my head lies the burden.
Some eat of the body, some take a stance.

NEIL FLEMING

'I thought, He has been alone in the wilderness for too long, and has become two people.' – Patrick deWitt, *The Sisters Brothers* (2011)

If there actually is a process, then it comes in two parts, and without the instructions.

First (usually) there is something that wants to be said. And then there is a seed. Without the seed, nothing can happen, because the poem builds up on it like a raindrop sticking to a bit of dust.

For instance: a single self-inventing phrase. *Floyd and Sookie pass out cigarettes.* (Who are *they*? I still don't know.) Or for another instance: there was a time when I couldn't write anything, and to get out of it, asked my youngest daughter to make up titles which I was then obliged to use. *The Gypsy's Chandelier. Clock with Brass Winding Key.*

Also there are stories. Some with pirates.

The something that wants to be said doesn't care, in the end. It will consume fuel of any kind. Phrase, title, rhythm, cadence, rhyme. It will make words take risks and spring surprises. Or compel some dull polysyllable to yield its secrets. *Industrious. Vectoring. Molecule. Furniture.* Rhyme schemes, strange ones in particular, feel like maps or guidebooks. Even if all the rhymes get chopped out later, the presence of rules can help uncover the unexpected. The world turns into something else.

And although these poems are filled with mornings and rooks and dogs and Suffolk and pieces of Africa, it is not that I was trying to *transcribe* them. The natural world is a laboratory, and a place for discussions with my childhood self; it's a wonder, and a sort of reproach.

New Year's Eve

A man came up the hill towards us, along the side of the field,
His dog shining beside him in the last light of the Year 2011.
A basket of rooks hung in an oak tree, instead of its missing leaves,
And fell out laughing as the dog went past and the moon rose.

As regards balance, nothing quite lives up to these kinds of days:
The wood-fire starting in the belly of the clouds, the stationary satellite
    opposite,
The rolling world and the invisible bronze galaxy sideways overhead,
The day's door closing, the year easing shut like a hatch.

A man came up the hill towards us, along the side of the field,
Treading the same line he did a hundred years ago, or two hundred,
Which was during the Napoleonic Wars, and also the year of the Great
    Comet,
Unfortunately not scheduled to re-visit these skies until AD 4907.

Sometimes you can stand just at the junction between farmland and
    heathland,
And the Scots pines a mile off will make it all look like Africa suddenly.
Everything's made of chalk: moon, sky, geography; thoughts about
    thoughts.
Sometimes you can stand right at the line between now and afterwards.

Paul McNeil Hill

All afternoon it rains on England out of whale-black clouds.
But it's May, so my fields and woods are also lit by turns,
And finally around six we see our chance, and walk.

I wear that mountain coat you left here by accident,
And which we kept and used because we always knew
You'd come back sooner or later to collect it.

The dog on the other hand just wears a dog-like grin,
Composed from smells and memories of smells,
And from the shape of running, from being alongside.

Sometimes I think he thinks it's really you. But then
I've often unexpectedly thought it's you myself: a voice,
A wind-lit shadow keeping pace in the high hills,

Something unspoken, spoken at crossing-points –
Ease, probably. Also the knowledge of wide day.
Nothing that ever any accident could take away.

Camber Sands

Most nights there's laughter in the dunes,
Even this late, the season almost up.
Stupid young kids, drawn here by god knows what,
Bacardi Breezers, sand in prophylactics,
Over the wire at Pontins, and away like vervets,
Lighting small fires, and September's big moon.

Only it's not that, really, is it.
Not when the tide's a sheet of bronze
And the cliff point beyond Rye glows black like fairyland.

Something else brings us; codgers at dawn,
Waterline pilgrims, and the faithful blind,
Metal-detectors with their metal detectors,
The lug-worm trolley and the trolley's tracks.
Also the boy with the inflatable shark.

It's the sea, dummy. It's the homely sea
That will clean everything, take everything,
Forgive all sins, erase all prints.
That's what it is.
It's the sea edge, where we have all sat
Since the invention of the universe and all dominions,
Frowning and wondering at hope's horizon.

Clock with Brass Winding Key

I bought yours in the soukh in Sharjah, remember,
From a thin shop with stuff right up the stairs:
Daggers, mostly, bits of elephants, and coffee pots.

The owner smelled of cinnamon. Mind you, everything
Was part-cinnamon back then, even the red sand,
Which crept constantly at night into the babies' cots.

How the damn clock got that far, God alone knows.
Made in Japan, it says, in Nineteen Twenty-Three,
Mostly out of wood, hand-painted tin, and lack of doubt.

But everything was in English: Favourite Watch Co,
Fifteen Years Guarantee. Eighty-six years on,
Still ticks comfortably. They must have turned them out

With Singapore in mind, for planters, smoking concerts,
The Straits Settlements, maybe as far west as Calcutta,
For the leather-faced conquerors, always from colder farms.

Business is business. Belongs in some Waiting Room,
Some dead-end branch line somewhere high: tea growing, mist.
Somehow the old thing made it farther, past the palms,

All the way past the tired pirates, past the shimmering coast,
On, on, to the dusk-glad harbour. Cargo. Oriental provenance.
Some good pieces. But still not this one really after all.

These days, it hangs on a wall four hundred years older,
In England, among snow and rain, fields and ditches.
You could imagine this as home, somewhere to stay.

But really it's about explaining what happened once,
And about what will happen later on, long beyond
Anything we might guess now. About the hours till it's day.

Diagnosis

They've just told you, and quite unexpectedly
Your mind walks out of your head and stands
On the other side of the room, frowning.

Somewhere else, a duck makes its way over a lake;
There are stationary locomotives in sidings,
Their beautiful lights still on, in the morning.

The doctor uses doctor's words, going fast,
Hoping to get past the shadow at the edge.
One of your two selves asks: *What have I just been told?*

They will tell you a second time, leaving out nothing,
Stepping carefully on every gaudy hope
As a woodsman treads out camp-fire embers.

The word means: insight, 'knowledge that goes through'.
But through you goes only rage and flames
That are both dread, and the defiance of dread –

Those two tall gentlemen who have supervised
All history, how we came out of the dark,
And how we still fight it, always and everywhere.

Later the same day, you step outside and find
Buildings and trees have taken up new positions.
Someone industrious has scrubbed the world with light.

Double History

Floyd and Sookie pass out cigarettes;
Everyone takes a breather.
It's hot as a chimney, has been since first light
Somewhere in the valley
A river ladles from pool to pool.

Every so often, when it least ought,
Something knocks on the inside of the vault.
The gate in the wall for once is unlocked,
And an apple garden is just off the street.
Someone's left a basket on the path.

History is what history begets:
A cover story usually, neither
The image nor the memory of sight,

A lightless alley,
Something they do at school.

Not this, this seismograph of thought.
Sudden adjustment in the fault:
The surprise of taking a wound; the heart rocked;
A voice that says: 'This happened'; sandalled feet
In the stairwell; someone running a bath.

Here's the wood where they really killed the King.
Here's the town they set on fire from the sky.
Here's where the stone belongs.
Someone stood here on this corner smiling,
Watching real Romans with real swords marching by
Whistling Latin songs.

Towelling Dry

We all held hands as far as the lake's edge and then
You walked in until it was up to your shoulders, where you stood
Looking around you at the brown water's lap, at intersecting rings
        of light
And the smudge of blue trees on the opposing shore.

For which reason we are now here: the woman in the water,
Elapsed time swaying about her, and the rest of us
On the bank, shadows behind us, conversation
Audible at some distance, everything clearly lit except
For this circumstance, which is you there and us here.

We are pretending if we talk for long enough
Then you will turn and wade out shaking off rain
And towel dry and dress and walk back across the fields.

Except that really we are both expecting something else
And you will turn and swim beyond earshot
Beyond the skim of a stone into open water where it is
As wide as the traverse between two stars,
Poised over fathoms of clear glass.

September's done

September's done. The elevated sky
Burns blue like gas jets. And me and the dog,
Both dipped in ochre, go over the stubble
And along the edge of the wood,
Lamp-lit with hawthorn berries, blackberries,
And, by the fence, this one wild apple tree,
Well-fruited, strung with globes, which says
There was a house once, in under there
Among the snickering wings, among
The green maze.

After some time, a slow-rowing heron comes past
Filled with disdain for earthbound things,
Angling over the field to where the road
Dips to the ford, and the dog chases him
Along the ground and in and out of shadow.
These things of no significance are turned
By autumn's sly approach to something else,
Arrival, maybe, or an assembly of light,
A bit like meaning, anyway.

Hartland Point

An envelope of mist up here, and a cream sea under the cliff,
Four gulls twenty feet off the geometry, vectoring,
Sea-roof patrol, slideways, nothing to report, no fish anyhow.

Somewhere down there you can hear the lighthouse singing,
Sitting under the headland, dressed entirely in pearls,
Patched into history, calling them all back, over and over.

What I like is that they thought this up, they wanted it
Enough to climb down, morning after morning, carrying stones,
And build a tower in the grey-green roar, the sloping.

Each one was dangerous, each one took years and lives.
Promising starts would wash away; so would the careless.
They did it for the drowned to be undrowned. For love, really.

Anyway sometimes after a hard day you'd get a sunset.
You could sit on the rocks and smoke a pipe,
Looking at Lundy Island, hoping for porpoises.

Sorry for your loss

I don't feel loss. Nothing is lost, you fools.
I'm only crying because this boat won't stop,
I'm only sad because the running sea's so deep.

I want those clouds repealed,
These stars rewound,
I want this ocean lit exclusively by hanging planets
Larger and better than moons.

Perhaps then we might strike land again,
And come ashore at Leigh,
And go by Kinder Scout, and Arnton Fell, and Applecross,

Or walk the Ring of Mourne together –
Windy Gap, the Hare's Gap – see
Green Donard shrug the slow mist from his flank
Very early one summer morning, very long ago.

Fortingall

It was probably a day just like today
The day they brought him down from off the hill.
You can imagine how his knees stuck up wax-white
From the birch-branch litter whipped together
Out of the last tree that he ever cut
And his eyes that were so blue all gone into slush.

Just like today: clouds piled like dirty snow,
The hissing sun unseen that starts a burning in the sky,
The wind off the mountains taking the smoke,
And the blue bite of the river when the boys
Climbed down together to pull up a big stone for him
Bigger than he was anyway lying there.

So then they turned the holy man out of his cot
And made him come down to the chapel
Even though it was by now raining across the glen.
No one knew the prayers, not even the holy man,
Who couldn't write his name it was so long ago
And so many dead already since the Spring.

But after they dug the hole and put the stone on him,
One of them came back the next day and the next
And since they couldn't give him the axe to sleep with
Cut its shape instead deep in the granite stone
To show what his father had done and how he lived
No one knows when.

Marvels: the yew tree has been here
Four thousand years, and probably is really
The oldest tree in Europe. And a daft story tells
How a Roman envoy and his wife,
Touring up north of the border,
Stopped here because the baby was early,
And named it Pontius Pilate. Also
The mound is still there in the flat field

Where the old woman leading her white horse
Buried the whole village after the plague.

But better than all of these on a day like today
Is to stand in the churchyard by his stone
And hear him singing and the iron ring
Of his axe high in the woods in October.

The Gypsy's Chandelier

Electric lamps illuminate
The terrace and the trees behind,
Where unsurprisingly we find
The chauffeur of the potentate
Asleep under the gate.

This isn't silence. There's a shade
Of traffic from the boulevard.
A lone cicada in the yard
Pipes midnight. Everything is made
Of molecules of jade.

French windows, opening, impose
An amber flag along the grass.
Four bars of conversation pass.
A man comes with a large pink rose
Rehearsing as he goes.

That's her new raincoat on the chairs,
Balloon glass on the balustrade.
Her lovers, and the friends just made,
Are gathered by the pantry stairs
Extemporising airs.

Nothing is said and nothing spent.
That which occurs is what occurs.
Somebody finds a shoe. It's hers.
The lantern and its filament
Irradiate what's meant.

Why don't we just get out of here,
And ditch the mermaid and the priest.
Somewhere slightly south of east
The foreshore burns before the feast,
Portents and wonders will appear,
Orion's dog will fire the year,
The gypsy's chandelier.

Lamu

By the mangrove jetty sits the Captain
And all his bad teeth
Shine in the sun like ivory because
That's what they're made of.
They shine by moonlight and under oil lamps
Because of smiling
Constantly upon the Indian Ocean.

Someone has thoughtlessly left a cannon
On the waterfront
For two hundred years. But it doesn't work,
Luckily for you.
He'd make his own gunpowder if he could
And sling cannonballs
All day long booming over the green deep.

He married this boat a long time ago,
And night after night
He sleeps with his imaginary niece
On bosomy swells,
And dreams of navigation, oranges,
And a clean salt wind
That will put everything back as it was

Before flying-boats, before photographs,
Before Diet Coke,
Before the military policemen,
Before kerosene.
Then he'll haul up his mast and all unfurled
Triangulate south
Using those teeth as some sort of compass.

ISABEL GALLEYMORE

Search for the etymology of the word *metaphor* and you'll find fragments of Old French, Latin and Greek, which, when translated, mean 'to carry over', 'to bear'. When I visualise these definitions, I can't help seeing the former as a husband carrying his wife over the threshold, the latter as a more burdensome relationship – perhaps one marked by imposition. 'Odd how a thing is most itself when likened,' Richard Wilbur remarked. But how is that thing also compromised through comparison?

This question looms largest in my mind when I'm writing about animals. Given the way it foists a human agenda onto nonhuman others, anthropomorphism is sometimes considered a dirty word. Yet, I'm curious as to how these figurative devices can stray from cats in bow-ties and bananas in pyjamas in order to create intimacy as well as estrangement. Perhaps because of these interests, much of my writing starts with research. 'Kind', for example, emerged from a day spent at an owl sanctuary where many owls have become 'imprinted': a term used, in this case, for animals who become so familiar with humans that they begin to take on certain human behaviours. Likewise, 'A Note' was influenced by my reading on bees: in particular, their practice of leaving pheromones to mark used sources of nectar.

A False Limpet

Armour tailored to an elbow's point and wrinkle, and with that
same toothy colour: a *False Limpet* by this encyclopedia – as if it were
never itself, only the imitation of something else. *It's the way you hold
your mouth so tight; you're so like someone I once met* – but O, watch this
slip from the rock with a splashy unclinginess.

At First

The seasons grew untidy;
the months filled up with rain.
At first it came soft as a sheep.
Inside the sheep a wolf, of course
inside the wolf a man intent
on acting out his tale.

The Ash

like a single branch of ash
honed to the handle of an axe
and made to take the hand
of a woodsman as he throws
his body weight to fell
all the ash has sown,
I turn your words although
the line you spoke was simple

My Heart's

When he says my heart's a jumper
caught on something sharp
like a pheasant hung from the rafters –
its breast a break-light in the dark,
the dark like the dark inside the mouth
of someone singing, and the song
briskly walked along by breath
the way the wind will walk a storm
in a pair of flared, fraying jeans
beyond the hills, the aspen wood
where trees are statues honouring
the sun, which like affection, seems
so rare these shrinking days, I think
my heart is not enough for him.

The Spiny Cockle

From their metre-deep sandy resorts
the waves have raised these hard orbs:
clenched like cement hedgehogs
they wear their ribs inside out
and pricked with a white picket fence
to keep their soapdish interiors –
their lattice-gill-slither selves –
from the crunch of an oystercatcher's kiss
or the orange fog of this starfish
that causes one cockle to buckle and let
its long pink foot slip like a leg
from the slit of its crenulated skirt:
soft pogo on which it floppy-leaps
away across the wet desert.

The Ocean

Wasn't walking beside her
walking with the ocean below
when you didn't know her and wanted to?
In that heat, along that path
you hesitated

at a slug, beached
like a tiny grey whale –
thirty tonnes and seventy years
of navigating the continental shelf
assumed by this soil-scuffing inch

and what would she make of you?
The ocean blinked.
Say you took that step, or say you fell,
wouldn't she move you miles in herself?

Together

the heart aflame no longer
shines any light on love
because they are always together –

because they are always together
it's hard to see them apart
like the blade in the blade of grass –

two lovers grew so close they became
too fluently familiar
having lost what makes fire fire.

And One Unlucky Starling

It would climb from its dirt-tank and whip
after dad's thrown oven chips –
and when it was full it would rest in the glare
of the TV like a drainpipe choked with moss
and one unlucky starling. Rare
was the sight of mum stroking it
as one of her own stockinged legs,
more often dad laid it over himself
as one of her stockinged legs –
still, it would nuzzle no one save me
and follow me to bed, my one-limbed teddy
they'd later call my tape measure
comparing its hungry length to mine
as into sleep I glided like a chip across the room.

A Squirrel

smears herself with snakeskin,
wears the perfume of its scales –

near hungry mouths she's invisible
as if she were another venomous tail.

Behind a tree somebody hid
but no one is exactly sure

if this is hiding or imitating
the yew, unmoving, lichen-furred.

And when you lie beneath his skin
what are you thinking, if you think at all?

Is it that you're half of him –
at one and indivisible?

or covering your breasts and thighs –
his body being the warmest hide?

Tended

A hot afternoon and tiredness has him
turning to the garden for fresh air
where he spills coffee and goes to swear – and swears
because she is, of course, in bed
and not about to come downstairs.

Beyond the oak, in full sun the fields
of maize grow rainbows as the tractors spray.

Beneath her curtained window, in their plot,
tended by his hands these days,
a bee is abandoning itself on his abandoned spade.

From the corner of his eye, he sees her
raise her claw as if to wave.

How long now? He blows away the steam and sips.
The struggling buzz of the bedside bell.
It no longer seems like myth; that those
who devote their lives to one another
like bee to blossom, blossom fruit,
will take their leave in the same hour.

I'm doing you an injustice

It's like I've invited you to a party
of people I know but you don't –
I see you fitting into the erratic
spaces between people talking
till I only see parts of you
like the nude beneath the willow
she doesn't look quite herself
dappled by the shadowings
from what is given light first.

The Crickets

With this breeze
the springing crickets explore
an astronaut's grasp of gravity. Flung

like the second half of a metaphor
I look back and there I am
and here, too

differently. Uncrossable
space between myselves.
A crowd

of moonwalkers tittering
and not one cricket
on the breeze.

Seahorse

Isn't it shocking how he speaks for her?
His voice across the restaurant –
she'll have the cod artichoke bake.

A giggle of bubbles comes from behind them:
a fish tank curtained with seagrass
where a seahorse is tying itself
to one of these slim, tweedy forms

like a hand shaping itself inside another's
the way my hand tucks into his
like a difference pretending it's not.

Nuptials

One day, downhill from the farmer's field,
I, a frog, married a drain,
married its cool and its damp,
web-wed its steely gills,
its shaggy walls and mind of flies:
to which the drain gave consent
silently adding its nuptials.

So overgrown with green
and happy clamminess,
on the eve of our first year
a fifth foot bulbed from my skin
with something of the pressure and shape
of a cork being eased
from a bottle of champagne.

All night, my croak in the air
was the closest I could get to your
– remind me, what do you call them –
fireworks or flares?

Kind

The owl anthropomorphises
himself upon the plinth,

being steeped
in his keeper's routine –

if we put a female in with him
he'd still make love with the hats on our heads –

he's been here twice as long as I've been
captivated by you,

like him I don't think of myself
as possessed

until one night, loosed to the world,
I find myself expecting

everyone to be your kind
of kindness.

A Note

A note on the petal
from the last nectar-robber –
I was here and drained the lot.

Others near and read
and reel sharply back
into the sky.

No matter, what he wrote
wears off – one flower
clothed in yellow claws

needs one full turn of Earth,
another dressed in blue
just minutes to re-self.

CONTRIBUTORS

Luke Allan is a poet and publisher. He is director of the small press Sine Wave Peak and managing editor of Carcanet Press. He co-edits the poetry journals *Pain*, *Butcher's Dog*, *Quait*, and *PN Review*. He received a Northern Promise Award for poetry in 2011. A pamphlet, *Minimum Soft Exchange*, was published by MIEL in 2016. He lives with his wife on a hill in West Yorkshire.

Zohar Atkins was born in Bearsville, New York, in 1988, and grew up in Montclair, New Jersey. He holds an A.B. in Classics and Jewish Studies and an A.M. in History from Brown University, and a DPhil in Theology from Oxford, where he was a Rhodes Scholar. A rabbinic student at the Jewish Theological Seminary, he is a Wexner Graduate Fellow and a Fellow at the David Hartman Center. His poem, 'Without Without Title' won the Oxonian Review Prize. His debut collection is forthcoming with Carcanet in 2019.

Rowland Bagnall was born in Oxfordshire in 1992. He studied English at St John's College, Oxford, and completed an MPhil in American Literature at the University of Cambridge. His poetry has previously appeared in various magazines, including *Poetry London*, *The Quietus*, and *PN Review*. He currently lives in Oxford. His first collection is forthcoming from Carcanet in 2019.

Sumita Chakraborty hails from Boston, Massachusetts and currently lives in Atlanta, Georgia. She holds a doctorate in English with a certificate in Women's, Gender, and Sexuality Studies from Emory University. Poetry editor of AGNI and art editor of *At Length*, her articles, essays and poems have recently appeared or are forthcoming in *Cultural Critique*, the *Los Angeles Review of Books*, *Poetry*, and elsewhere. In 2017 the Poetry Foundation awarded her a Ruth Lilly and Dorothy Sargent Rosenberg Fellowship.

Mary Jean Chan is a poet from Hong Kong. Her poems have appeared in *The 2018 Forward Book of Poetry*, *The Poetry Review*, *PN Review*, *The*

London Magazine, Oxford Poetry, Poetry London and *Ambit*. She won the 2017 Poetry Society Members' Competition, the 2017 Poetry and Psychoanalysis Competition and the 2016 Oxford Brookes International Poetry Competition (ESL). A poem of Chan's was shortlisted for the 2017 Forward Prize for Best Single Poem. As a PhD candidate and Research Associate at Royal Holloway, University of London, she won the 2017 PSA/Journal of Postcolonial Writing Postgraduate Essay Prize. She is a Co-Editor at *Oxford Poetry*. Her debut collection is forthcoming from Faber & Faber in 2019.

Helen Charman was born in 1993. She is writing a PhD thesis on maternity, sacrifice, and political economy in nineteenth-century fiction, and teaches undergraduates at the University of Cambridge and primary school children in Hackney, where she currently lives. Her critical writing can be found introducing the short stories of Mary Butts for the ANON series (Oxford: Hurst Street Press, 2017), in *The Cambridge Humanities Review, The King's Review* and elsewhere. She was shortlisted for *The White Review* Poet's Prize in 2017, and her first pamphlet of poems is forthcoming from Offord Road Books in 2018.

Rebecca Cullen studied English and Drama in Wales and Sheffield before working in Further Education and the Civil Service. She received a Distinction for an MA in Creative Writing at Nottingham Trent University in 2013. She is currently an NTU doctoral scholar, researching the relationship between poetry and time, funded by Midlands3Cities DTP and the AHRC. Her poems have appeared in journals such as PN *Review, The North* and *New Walk*, and she regularly leads poetry workshops across the community. Rebecca is also the host at Totally Wired early evening poetry.

Ned Denny was born in London in 1975 and has worked as a postman, art critic, book reviewer, music journalist and gardener. His poems and 'masks' have appeared in publications including PN *Review, Poetry Review, The White Review, Oxford Poetry, The TLS* and *Modern Poetry in Translation*. His first collection, *Unearthly Toys*, was published by Carcanet in 2018.

Neil Fleming is a poet, playwright, screenwriter, translator, software writer, and occasional energy markets consultant. He was educated at Trinity College, Cambridge, and the University of Vienna. A former journalist, he has lived and worked in Africa, the Middle East, Europe and the UK, covering wars, famines, elephants, politics, OPEC and the oil industry. In 2002 he co-founded the theatre company Hydrocracker. Three of his plays – *Musik, The Consultant,* and *Wild Justice* – have been produced in London, Plymouth and Brighton. He won the 2005 Kent and Sussex Poetry competition. He lives in Suffolk and is married with three grown-up daughters.

Isabel Galleymore is a lecturer at the University of Birmingham. Her debut pamphlet, *Dazzle Ship,* was published in 2014 by Worple Press. Her work has featured in *Poetry, Poetry London* and *Poetry Review,* among other magazines. In 2016, she was Poet in Residence at the Tambopata Research Centre in the Amazon rainforest. She received an Eric Gregory Award in 2017.

Katherine Horrex was born in Liverpool and grew up in Hull, where she studied, before moving to Manchester. Her poems have been published in the *The TLS, Morning Star,* PN *Review, Poetry London, Poetry Salzburg Review* and *The Poetry Business Introduction* X; they are forthcoming in *Some Cannot Be Caught: The Emma Press Book of Beasts.* She holds an MA from Manchester University's Centre for New Writing.

Lisa Kelly is half deaf and half Danish. She is the Chair of *Magma Poetry* and co-edited issue 63, The Conversation Issue; and issue 69, The Deaf Issue. She is a regular host of poetry evenings at the Torriano Meeting House, London and has an MA in Creative Writing with Distinction from Lancaster University. Her pamphlet *Bloodhound* is published by Hearing Eye. She is currently a freelance journalist, and has worked as an actress, life model, Consumer Champion, waitress, sales assistant and envelope stuffer. Her pamphlet *Philip Levine's Good Ear* is forthcoming from Stonewood Press in 2018.

Born in Singapore, **Theophilus Kwek** has published four volumes of poetry – most recently *The First Five Storms*, which won the New Poets' Prize in 2016. He has also won the Berfrois Poetry Prize and the Jane Martin Prize, and was placed Second in the Stephen Spender Prize for poetry in translation. His poems, translations and essays have appeared in *The Guardian, The North, The London Magazine, Cha, The Irish Examiner,* and *The Philosophical Salon.* He previously served as President of the Oxford University Poetry Society, and is now Co-Editor of *Oxford Poetry* as well as Editor-at-Large for Singapore at *Asymptote.*

Andrew Latimer is an editor, publisher and writer. He is editorial director at Little Island Press and founding editor of *Egress.*

Toby Litt was born in 1968 and grew up in Ampthill, Bedfordshire. He is the author of ten novels, including *deadkidsongs, Ghost Story* and *Notes for a Young Gentleman,* and four short story collections. His most recent book is *Wrestliana,* a memoir about his great-great-great grandfather, William Litt – a champion wrestler, poet, smuggler and exile. He lectures in Creative Writing at Birkbeck, University of London.

James Leo McAskill was born in Manchester and studied in Glasgow. He is an editor at Little Island Press. He lives in Lisbon.

Rachel Mann is an Anglican parish priest and honorary canon of Manchester Cathedral. She is the author of four books including a best-selling theological memoir of growing up trans, *Dazzling Darkness.* Formerly Poet in Residence at Manchester Cathedral, her poems have been published in PN Review, *The North, Magma,* and other places. Her current book is *Fierce Imaginings: The Great War, Ritual, Memory & God* (DLT, 2017).

Jamie Osborn founded Cambridge Student PEN and for two years was poetry editor at *The Missing Slate.* His translations of Iraqi refugee poems have appeared in *Modern Poetry in Translation* and *Botch,* and his own poems in *Blackbox Manifold, New Welsh Review, Lighthouse,* BODY and elsewhere. He has also published translations from the German of Jan Wagner. He lives in Brussels.

Andrew Wynn Owen is a Fellow by Examination at All Souls College, Oxford. He received the university's Newdigate Prize in 2014 and an Eric Gregory Award from the Society of Authors in 2015. With the Emma Press, he has published pamphlets including a narrative poem, lyrics, and a collaboration (with John Fuller).

Phoebe Power received an Eric Gregory Award from the Society of Authors in 2012 and a Northern Writers' Award in 2014. A live version of her pamphlet, *Harp Duet* (Eyewear, 2016) was recently performed with electronic music, and her current project, *Christl*, is a collaboration between four artists in poetry, visual art and sound. Her first collection, *Shrines of Upper Austria*, was published by Carcanet in 2018. She lives in York.

Michael Schmidt is a founder of Carcanet Press and its Managing and Editorial Director. He is General Editor of the magazine PN *Review* and has been involved in editing all seven *New Poetries*.

Laura Scott grew up in London but now lives in Norwich. Her poems have appeared in various magazines including PN *Review* and *Poetry Review*. She won the Geoffrey Dearmer Prize in 2015 and the Michael Marks Prize for her pamphlet *What I Saw*. She was commended in the 2017 National Poetry Competition.

Vala Thorodds is an Iceland-born poet, publisher, editor, translator, and literary curator. She is the founding director of Partus, an independent literary press based in Reykjavík and Manchester. Her poetry has recently been published in print and online in *The White Review*, *Poetry Wales*, *Gutter*, *Ambit*, *Magma* and *Hotel*. She has published one chapbook in Icelandic, *What Once Was Forest* (2015), and her nonfiction articles have appeared on or in *Dazed*, *Cereal*, *Iceland Review*, and *The Reykjavík Grapevine*. Her translations of the icelandic poet Kristín Ómarsdóttir are forthcoming from Carcanet in 2018.

ACKNOWLEDGEMENTS

Luke Allan: 'Sic Transit Gloria Mundi' and 'Pennyweight' appeared in *Oxford Poetry*. 'A Note on Walking to Elgol' and 'The grace of a curve...' in *Magma*. 'Advice of the Assistant in a Card Shop...' and 'Alexandrine' in *The Rialto*. 'The true path is...' in *Quait*. 'Love Poem' in *Lighthouse*. 'The grace of a curve...' borrows words from Gaston Bachelard and 'The Road Not Taken' from Robert Frost.

Zohar Atkins: 'System Baby' appeared in TYPO. 'Without Without Title' in the *Oxonian Review*. 'Song of Myself (Apocryphal)', 'Fake Judaism', 'Déjà Vu' and 'The Binding of Isaac' in PN *Review*.

Sumita Chakraborty: 'Dear, beloved' appeared in *Poetry*.

Mary Jean Chan: poems appeared in PN *Review*, *The London Magazine*, *The Rialto*, *English: Journal of the English Association* and *Poetry News* (The Poetry Society).

Helen Charman: 'Angiogram', 'The Roses of Heliogabalus' and 'Thin girls' appeared online in *Hotel*. 'Tampon panic attack' in *Blackbox Manifold*. 'Type F (captive / voluntary)' and 'Type C (fiscal)' in *Datableed*, 'Agony in the Garden' on the MINERVA *platform*.

Ned Denny: 'Drones' appeared in *The White Review*.

Isabel Galleymore: 'The Ash' and 'Seahorse' appeared in *Poetry*. 'A False Limpet' in *Stand*. 'A Note' in *Triptychs* (Guillemot Press). 'Together' and 'I'm Doing You an Injustice' in *Dazzle Ship*.

Katherine Horrex: 'Four Muses', Grey Natural Light' and 'Goat Fell' appeared in PN *Review*. 'Polycystic' in *Introduction X: The Poetry Business Book of New Poets*. 'Lapwings in Fallowfield' and 'Brexit' in *Manchester Review*.

Lisa Kelly: 'Apple Quartet' appeared in PN *Review*. 'Trailing Spouse' and 'A Map Towards Fluency' in *Ambit*. 'Out of Order' won Lancaster

University's open competition on Reading (MA Category), 'A Desultory Day' in The Rialto. 'Anonymous' in Prole. 'A Chorus of Jacks in 13 Texts' and 'Cuddles are Drying up Like the Sun in a Data Lake' in Tears in the Fence. 'The Dogs of Pénestin' was longlisted for the 2016 National Poetry Competition.

Theophilus Kwek: poems appeared in The Adroit Journal, Asia Literary Review, Berfrois, Eastlit, Irish Literary Review, The London Magazine, The Missing Slate, PN Review and Wildness. 'Camerata' was a runner-up in the Fish Poetry Prize 2016, and appeared in the prize anthology of that year. 'Occurrence' appeared in Flight, an anthology in response to the Syrian refugee crisis. '24.6.2016', 'Occurrence', 'Requiem' and 'Road Cutting at Glanmire' appeared in The First Five Storms (smith|doorstop, 2017).

Toby Litt: Life Cycle premiered at the Women of the World Festival, Southbank, 2011. It also featured in the Norfolk & Norwich Festival and was performed at the Howard Assembly Room, Leeds. Support in developing the cycle came from Opera North. The performers were Mara Carlyle (voice), John Reid (piano) and Oliver Coates (cello) in a staging by Netia Jones. The lyrics to Life Cycle were published, online, by flexipress, edited by Richard Brammer and Ferdinand Beckett. 'Stillborn', 'Amnio', 'The gap so small', 'Not just milk' and 'The first turn' were part of Life Cycle.

James Leo McAskill: 'Coming Thunder' appeared in the The London Magazine. 'Days', 'The Norseman's First Summer' and 'Labour' in PN Review.

Andrew Wynn Owen: 'What Matters', 'The Borderline' and 'Till Next Time' appeared online in Tower Poetry. 'The Rowboat' was published online by Girton College, Cambridge, as part of the Jane Martin Poetry Competition.

Phoebe Power: Poems appeared in The Rialto, Poems Underwater, The Quietus, Oxford Poetry and Harp Duet (Eyewear, 2012).

Laura Scott: 'If I could write like Tolstoy' and 'The Dogs in Greece are different' appeared in *Poetry Review*. 'The Singing' in *The Rialto*. 'Fence' in *Oxford Poetry*. 'and Pierre?', 'To the Trees' and 'So Many Houses' in PN *Review*. 'Tolstoy's Dog' and 'Turner' are in *What I Saw* (Rialto). 'What the trees do' was highly commended in the 2017 Resurgence Prize and is published on the Poetry School's website.

Vala Thorodds: 'Enemies' and 'Through Flight' appeared online in *The White Review*. 'Inertia' and 'in' appeared in *Gutter*. 'Aperture' and 'The Difference' are translated from the Icelandic and appeared in *SAND* (Berlin). 'Rain' was commissioned by the film journal *Fireflies*, where it appeared in an earlier form. 'Luck' appeared in *Poetry Wales*. 'Carelessly We Have Entangled Ourselves' and 'Naked Except for the Jewellery' (which takes its title from a poem by Jack Gilbert) appeared in *Ambit*.